WORCESTER
A Pictorial History

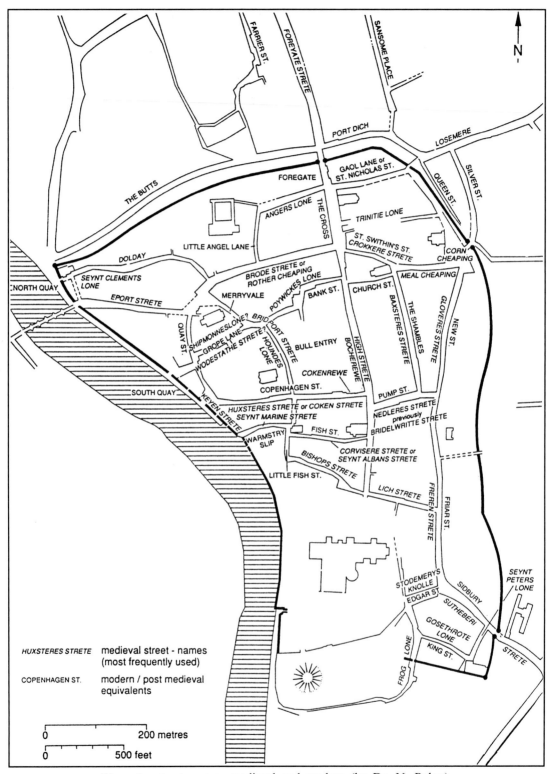

Worcester street-names—medieval and modern (by Dr. N. Baker).

WORCESTER
A Pictorial History

Tim Bridges
and
Charles Mundy

Phillimore

1996

Published by
PHILLIMORE & CO. LTD.,
Shopwyke Manor Barn, Chichester, West Sussex

ISBN 0 85033 990 1

Printed and bound in Great Britain by
BIDDLES LTD.
Guildford, Surrey

*This book is dedicated to
the citizens of Worcester—past, present and future*

List of Illustrations

Frontispiece: Medieval and modern street names

Maps and Views of Worcester

1. Plan of medieval Worcester and its suburbs
2. Map of Worcester in the second quarter of the 19th century
3. Plan of Worcester, 1808
4. Speed's map of Worcester, 1610
5. Worcester from the west in the 1750s
6. Worcester from the west in the 18th century
7. Worcester Cathedral, before 1819
8. Worcester from New Road, 1828
9. Worcester from Hallow, 1879
10. Worcester from Diglis, 1883
11. Worcester from Diglis after 1815
12. Worcester from the south-west in the early 19th century
13. Worcester from the north-east in the early 19th century
14. Worcester from the north-east, 1829

River and Bridge

15. S.S. *Worcester*, South Quay
16. Droitwich salt trow, 1883
17. 'Great Flood', 1886
18. Long netting, *c*.1925
19. River Severn, 1932
20. The medieval bridge, before 1781
21. Worcester bridge, 1810
22. Worcester bridge, 1910
23. The tollhouses, Worcester bridge, 1931
24. A table of tolls
25. The Watermen's Church
26. A boat trip on the Severn in the 1930s
27. Worcester Cathedral from the bridge
28. Diglis weir
29. Diglis weir in the 1930s
30. The confluence of the rivers Severn and Teme

The Cathedral Area

31. Worcester Cathedral from Chapter Meadows
32. The west end of the cathedral
33. The monastic infirmary, 1873
34. Cathedral Precincts from the west, 1834 and 1870

35. The north porch, 1858
36. The Watergate, 1881
37. The crypt, 1844
38. The chapter house
39. Passage to the cloisters, 1844
40. The monastic treasury, 1844
41. By the monastic treasury, 1844
42. The Guesten Hall, 1844
43. The Guesten Hall in the late 19th century
44. The Deanery kitchen, 1844
45. Back of the Deanery, 1844
46. Chapter house and Guesten Hall, 1844
47. College Hall in the 19th century
48. College Hall in the early 20th century
49. The prebendal houses, College Green
50. Edgar Tower, 1781
51. Old St Michael's Church, *c*.1800

Lychgate

52. The line of College Street, plan 1794
53. St Michael's Church and College Street, 1938
54. The Lich Gate
55. The Lich Gate, 1878
56. 22 Lich Street, 1902
57. Lich Street, 1901
58. Lich Street, 1904

High Street

59. South end of High Street in the 1930s
60. South end of High Street, 1860
61. St Helen's Church, 1878
62. The Market Hall, *c*.1853
63. Sigley's China, 1910
64. Guildhall, 1901
65. Guildhall, 1911

Friar Street and north-east to Lowesmoor

66. Friar Street, *c*.1800
67. Greyfriars, Friar Street, 1896
68. Friar Street in 1931 looking north
69. Number 13 Court, Friar Street, 1903
70. New Street in the 19th century
71. 14-15 The Shambles, 1890

72. 13 The Shambles in the early 20th century
73. Queen Elizabeth House before 1891
74. Queen Elizabeth House after 1891
75. Sansome Street, 1975
76. Sansome Street and Lowesmoor, 1975
77. Trinity in the 19th century
78. The Music Hall, Cornmarket, c.1853
79. The Three Choirs Festival, the Public Hall, 1905
80. Sigley's and E.H. Quinton, 1980
81. Fownes Glove Factory, c.1890
82. St Paul's Church before 1988
83. St Peter's Sunday School, Lock Street, before c.1971
84. A cottage in Little Park Street in 1926
85. 22 Lowesmoor, 1904
86. Exhibition building, Shrub Hill Road

The City Wall

87. The city walls
88. The city walls, 1833
89. The city walls by Old St Martin's Church, 1878
90. City Walls Road under construction, 1975
91. Across the line of the city walls, 1975
92. Talbot Street, looking south, 1975
93. The southern end of City Walls Road under construction, 1975
94. Across the line of the city walls to Sidbury, 1975

The Sidbury Area

95. Junction of Sidbury and Edgar Street, c.1930
96. Angel Court, Sidbury, 1902
97. Severn Street, 1905
98. 44 Severn Street in 1935
99. King Street in 1935
100. King Street in 1935
101. The church of St Peter the Great, 1835, from the south west
102. The church of St Peter the Great, 1835, from King Street
103. St Peter's Street in the 1890s
104. The rebuilt church of St Peter the Great, 1976, from King Street
105. Diglis canal basin in the early 20th century
106. Fort Royal in the 19th century

The Commandery

107. Sidbury, 1839
108. The Commandery frontage, 1974
109. View from the Commandery canal wing, 1974
110. Exterior of the Great Hall between 1866 and 1887
111. The Commandery kitchens, 1974

112. No. 1 Commandery Drive, 1976
113. No. 1 Commandery Drive, 1974
114. The Commandery attic, 1974
115. The Commandery across the canal, 1974
116. The Commandery, terrace and canal, 1976

West of High Street and down to the River Severn

117. Fish Street, 1902
118. Birdport, 1904
119. Birdport and the junction with Grope Lane, 1898
120. North side of Copenhagen Street, 1904
121. St Andrew's Church and Copenhagen Street, 1912
122. The rear of Copenhagen Street in the 1930s
123. All Hallows in the 18th century
124. All Saints' Passage, 1892
125. Behind All Saints' Church, 1904
126. Houses to the north of All Saints' Church
127. The north side of All Saints' Church cleared
128. Inside All Saints' Church, 1904
129. Newport Street, 1905
130. Dolday, 1902
131. Dolday in 1931

The Cross, Foregate Street and into the north

132. The Cross, 1934
133. The Cross in the early 1900s
134. The Foregate, 1975
135. Foregate Street in the early 19th century
136. A bazaar at the Shire Hall
137. The public library and Hastings Museum, before 1896
138. The site of the Victoria Institute
139. The site of the Victoria Institute
140. The site of the Victoria Institute
141. Foregate Street elevation of the Victoria Institute, 1896
142. The art gallery at the Victoria Institute in the early 20th century
143. Porcelain display, Victoria Institute, early 20th century
144. The Shire Hall in the 19th century
145. 59 The Tything, 1892
146. 77 The Tything, 1908
147. The *Saracen's Head* bowling green in the 19th century
148. Springfield, Britannia Square, 1937
149. Little London, 1903
150. Little London under demolition

Outer Worcester

151. Tybridge Street and Hylton Road, c.1930
152. Grosvenor Walk, St John's, before 1979
153. Church Walk, St John's, 1977

154. St Clement's School, St John's, 1977
155. Bransford Road, St John's, 1910
156. The manor house of Hardwick, St John's
157. St George's Lane, Barbourne, 1905
158. Pitchcroft Lane, Barbourne, 1892
159. The Shrubbery in the late 19th century
160. The riverside by Pitchcroft

161. Old Worcester waterworks, Barbourne
162. Gheluvelt Park in the early 1920s
163. Northwick Cinema, 1938
164. Perdiswell Hall
165. The Old Turnpike, London Road
166. Royal Agricultural Society Show, Battenhall, 1863

Acknowledgements

The pictures illustrated here are from the collections of Worcester City Museum and Art Gallery, Foregate Street, Worcester, and we are most grateful to the Leisure Services Committee of Worcester City Council for making them available for publication. We would like to thank all our colleagues at the Museum for their support, in particular Iain Rutherford, Deborah Dean, Helen Sykes, Anna Dolecka and Garston Phillips, and we are indebted to Jeremy Pardoe for reproducing many of the illustrations. We are grateful to Dr. Nigel Baker for providing illustrations 1 and 2, and to Jean Peters and Angie Bishop for doing much of the typing. The advice of local history researchers Barbara Ronchetti, Joan Knowles and Annette Leech has been much appreciated.

The study of Worcester's past, having started perhaps with the records of the medieval monks, is a dynamic process which continually evolves as new documentary information is brought to light or archaeological discoveries are made. While we have attempted to provide an up-to-date summary of the city's history, this cannot hope to embrace all the themes and stories which Worcester has to tell—or which remain to be told—and our readers are therefore urged to use the Bibliography to further their interests and to draw their own conclusions. While numerous individuals have contributed to the study of the city's past, including the many local people who collate and research the city's archives, we would particularly like to mention the following whose academic work and thinking (most important of all) has provided the substance on which the early history of the settlement can presently be written: Dr. N. Baker, P. Barker, Dr. S. Bassett, C. Beardsmore, Professor M.O.H. Carver, H. Dalwood, Dr. C. Dyer, Dr. R. Holt, Dr. P. Hughes, J. Roberts, and Dr. D. Whitehead.

In addition to the academic contributions of these and many others, we would also like to acknowledge the efforts of the numerous archaeologists (volunteer and professional) who have toiled in often appalling conditions to salvage the objects and information on which much of the settlement's earlier history is based. During the 1970s and '80s much of this work was carried out by local young unemployed people on Community Programme Schemes (a number of whom are now working as professional archaeologists, some having gone on to university and obtained degrees) and, while these schemes were cut in 1988, Worcester's younger citizens continue to show their interest and enthusiasm for the city's past through the work they submit every year as part of the Worcester City History Awards scheme for schools. Long may this continue.

Introduction

The city of Worcester lies on the banks of the river Severn, just above its confluence with the Teme, about seven miles to the north-east of the Malvern Hills and about six miles to the south-west of Droitwich. The historic core of the settlement at Worcester developed on the east bank of the river, spreading northwards along an oblong sand and gravel river terrace which is overlooked by low-lying hills to the east (variously named Rainbow, Tallow, Merrimans, Shrub, Gorse, Elbury, Leopard, Lark, Catherine's—more recently called Fort Royal—Perry Wood and Red Hills). Water draining off this high ground once flowed in the Frog Brook, now part of the Birmingham and Worcester Canal, and together with its once marshy valley bottom this stream formed a natural eastern boundary for the early settlers. Suburban development later spread into this valley along roads running to Gloucester and Oxford/London, at Sidbury, and to Droitwich, at Lowesmoor, while a long sprawling suburb developed northwards along the city's main axial road which forks after the junction with Barbourne Brook towards Kidderminster and Droitwich. At the southern end of the river terrace, towards Diglis, the natural promontory created by the juncture between Frog Brook and the Severn provided an ideal defensive position for the early settlement, and this aspect is preserved today by the cathedral which dominates the location. To the south of this promontory lies Diglis basin and the river lock at Diglis Lock Island, while to the north, contained between a broad bend in the river and the river terrace, is the alluvial fan of Pitchcroft—the site of the present-day racecourse.

The present river bridge, which was opened in 1781, replaced a medieval stone structure (possibly of Roman origin) which lay some 150 metres upstream between Newport Street (east bank) and Tybridge Street (west bank). During the medieval period a man-made causeway originally carried traffic coming across this from the east up into the suburb of St John's, which sits on high ground formed by a sand and gravel river terrace mirroring that on the east bank. Extending between the St John's terrace and the river, from the bridge down to the junction with the river Teme, lies a broad alluvial plain which is subject to regular flooding (as are the Pitchcroft and Diglis areas). At the southern end of the St John's terrace, at Powick, there has been a bridge over the Teme since at least medieval times, linking Worcester to Great Malvern, while routes pass through St John's running north to Bewdley, north-west to Tenbury, and due west to Hereford and Leominster.

Looking down over the city from the Malverns it is easy to appreciate the strategic setting of the site. To the east and south east, relatively flat and low-lying land stretches towards the West Midlands plain and the Vale of Evesham, with the Cotswolds beyond, while to the west the hills and valleys of Herefordshire merge into the more mountainous country of the Clun and Radnor forests and, to the south west, the Forest of Dean and the Black Mountains. Winding its way down from the Severn Estuary (and Bristol) past Gloucester and Tewkesbury in a broad floodplain, the

Severn begins to narrow at Worcester before passing on through to Bewdley and Bridgnorth, with Shrewsbury ultimately beyond. Providing the most suitable bridging point between Bridgnorth and Gloucester until the 14th century, and with a six-foot tidal influence which made the river fordable at low tide until the construction of the Diglis locks in 1844, the strategic significance of the site can readily be appreciated. Of course for the early inhabitants of Worcester, living on the site of a strategic river-crossing would have had mixed blessings. While opportunities for trade and commerce have abounded, providing stimuli and markets to local manufacturers and farmers, the settlement has had to contend with numerous passing armies and war bands, many of which took the opportunity to stop off and plunder the settlement on their way through. Aside from these unwelcome visitors, the volume of traffic passing through the city has been a constant problem since at least the early 14th century, and remains one of the most important issues on the city's civic agenda today.

Following numerous medieval fires and sieges, Civil War bombardments, and a particularly rapacious spate of urban redevelopment in the 1960s and '70s, Worcester today retains few of its medieval buildings, and no structures are visible which pre-date the late Saxon period. While the city's medieval street pattern and city walls are still clearly visible, and the monastic ruins in the Cathedral Close and the Edgar Tower entrance to it hint at the city's medieval grandeur, the built environment of today is dominated by Georgian and Victorian architecture, with more recent structures blending or detracting from this in varying degrees. However, the 15th-, 16th- and 17th-century timber buildings which can still be seen in Friar Street, New Street, the Trinity and the Cornmarket do provide a glimpse of what the later medieval city may have been like, and many of the city's churches, including the cathedral, retain elements of their medieval fabric. Despite the lack of surviving structures we at least have documentary sources, cartographic and archaeological evidence to help us understand how the medieval town worked. For the origins and early development of the settlement, however, we must rely on archaeological evidence alone and it is to this that we now turn to begin the city's story.

The First Settlers

Washed down with the melting of the Irish Sea ice sheet, which reached its maximum extent north of Wolverhampton and west of Hereford c.42,000 B.C., the sand and gravel river terraces and ford at Worcester would have made an ideal location for prehistoric settlement. While the promontory and high ground on the east bank might have provided the more favourable location for defensive purposes, the critical factor for the early settlers may have been on which side of the river their allegiances lay. As the hills of Herefordshire, with the highland zone beyond, would have represented a significant barrier to settlers moving into the area from the east, there would have been distinct advantages to living on the west bank of the river in prehistoric times. However, while scatters of prehistoric flints, including some Palaeolithic material, are known from both sides of the river, there is presently no concrete evidence for any settlement sites dating to the earlier prehistoric periods other than for hints on Gorse Hill (Mesolithic and Bronze Age), in the city centre on the east bank (Bronze Age), and in the area of the medieval core of St John's (Mesolithic, Neolithic and Bronze Age).

If we are to look for a prehistoric origin for the settlement at Worcester, then on present evidence the late Iron Age provides the best candidate. Pottery, coins and a horse-burial (possibly ritual) from the period 150 B.C.—A.D. 43 have been found on excavations in the city centre on the east bank, and the remains of a late Iron-Age ditch and earth rampart, with settlement evidence inside, were briefly investigated during the 1960s in the area south of Pump Street, between the High Street and Friar Street, before being cleared to make way for a new shopping precinct, the Lychgate centre. While the totality of the evidence is poor, we can envisage a small farming community living on the east bank during the period prior to the Roman invasion, with a defended enclosure of less than eight hectares (20 acres) lying at the southern end of the river terrace. This community would have lived within the territory of the Dobunni, whose northern border lies along this stretch of the river Severn, and would no doubt have been subject to one of the much larger Iron-Age communities living in the Malvern hill-forts, or around Bredon Hill to the south.

The Roman Industrial Town, First - Fourth Centuries A.D.

When the Romans invaded Britain in A.D. 43 their military strategy relied as much upon building forts next to defended tribal centres as it did on winning set-piece battles. When the campaigning reached the Severn in the late 40s and 50s A.D., the 20th Legion built a road on the east bank of the river between the legionary fortresses at Kingsholm (near Gloucester) and Wroxeter (on the Severn near Shrewsbury). This road passed through Worcester, and has been identified on a number of archaeological sites in the northern part of the city (from Castle Street to Broad Street), running some 150 metres to the west of the present High Street/Tything alignment. The road has also been seen at Sidbury heading in the direction of Frog Brook, and from this junction it probably followed the line of Bath Road southwards towards Gloucester; the alignment still visible in the field boundaries to the south of Timberdine Farm. Whether or not a bridge was constructed over the river at this time is uncertain, although the site was presumably significant as a fording point, providing access to the Malvern hill-forts and the communities living beyond.

While there is evidence that the late Iron-Age defensive ditch on the east bank may have been dug out during the first century A.D., there is no other evidence to suggest that this was used as a fort by the Romans. The scatters of military equipment and coins found in the city centre from this early period may have been lost during the course of road building, or won by the local inhabitants in battle; they are not in themselves evidence of the presence of a Roman military garrison. North of the city, however, in the area of Perdiswell golf-course, a triple ditch enclosure has been identified by aerial photography, and this may be the remains of a Roman marching camp or fort—although whether this is Worcester's missing Roman fort remains to be tested.

As the Roman military machine passed across the Severn to begin campaigning in Wales, the military significance of the river crossing at Worcester would have faded, leaving the local inhabitants to adapt to the new economic and political conditions of the times. It was probably during this immediate post-conquest period that a branch road to the salt-producing centre at Droitwich was constructed—possibly following the line of an old prehistoric trackway—leading off the main highway through Lowesmoor, up Rainbow Hill and into the Warndon area. Salt is likely to have been brought along this to Worcester to be traded up and down the river.

While trade and commerce would have been a feature of the first-century settlement, which may have had a nucleated core in the area of the present Cathedral Close (within the old Iron-Age enclosure), the community was predominantly engaged with an agrarian economy exploiting the light tillable soils on the river terraces. Cattle pens, threshing floors and agricultural buildings from this period have been discovered in the present city centre, and while these are associated with Roman-style pottery and imported goods (such as high-quality Samian tableware from Gaul), it is not until the early second century that any sign of 'Roman' structure can be seen in the settlement layout.

The massive investment in capital works which took place in Britain during the first half of the second century A.D. (in particular during the reign of the Emperor Hadrian) provided a demand for raw materials, tools and manpower which stimulated economic development throughout the province, and it was probably this that prompted the development of a major iron smelting industry at Worcester. This industry seems to have begun in the Deansway/Broad Street area, where excavations have revealed three regularly laid-out streets associated with clay furnace bases and other structures forming part of a complex which extended northwards into Blackfriars (now the Friary Mall shopping centre) and Angel Place. During the course of the third century this complex grew northwards along the main road as far as Castle Street, a distance of over half a kilometre, and extended down as far as the river banks on Pitchcroft—an area of over sixteen hectares (approximately forty acres).

The massive scale of the iron workings provided an abundant supply of iron slag which was selectively used as a road surfacing material (the still iron-rich slag rusted together to form a true 'metalled' surface), and may well have been used for other civil engineering projects. Demolition of the medieval bridge in 1781 revealed iron slag piers that were removed with 'the utmost difficulty', suggesting that the structure may originally have been Roman, while bore-hole evidence indicates that the medieval Newport Street/Dolday suburb was built on an artificial tongue of land between the river terrace and the bridgehead which comprised, at its lower levels, a massive dump of iron slag. So extensive was this dump that in 1653 Andrew Yarranton was granted permission by the City Corporation to mine 'Roman cinders' from Pitchcroft (on the site of the present cattle market) which he re-smelted in the technologically more advanced furnaces of the time.

The ore for the industry probably came from a local source of bog iron—not the Roman mines in the Forest of Dean—while the charcoal fuel would have been produced locally. Although a massive amount of pig-iron was being produced by the settlement, it appears to have been transported elsewhere for manufacturing purposes, presumably mainly by river, which raises the question as to where the settlement's docking facilities were located. Aside from the waterfront of the east bank itself, the juncture of the Frog Brook with the Severn (at Diglis) would have provided a sufficiently deep off-channel harbouring facility, although as yet neither area has been investigated archaeologically.

While the second- and third-century Roman settlement is presently classed as a specialised industrial site, the area of the presumed town centre—the area of the later Cathedral Close—still remains to be investigated. This nucleus would probably have contained a market area, shops, taverns, domestic buildings and, possibly, a few public buildings, although the settlement was probably not an administrative centre during this period and does not appear to have been a formally planned Roman town. While limestone was imported from the Cotswolds, this appears to have been used mainly to line wells and make plaster (painted fragments of which are known from the city), and on the present evidence most of the settlement's buildings would appear to have been timber constructions. Suburban development extended into the Sidbury area, and here the third-century buildings benefited from a water supply provided by iron-collared wooden pipes. To the north of the industrial suburb, in Britannia Square, the footings of a circular sandstone building discovered in the 1840s may have been the remains of a Roman temple, and finds of roof tile and the occasional *tessera* (mosaic fragment) in the area certainly point to the existence of one or more high status Roman buildings there. While the settlement cemeteries have still to be located, Roman cremation burials are known south of Severn Street (south of the cathedral) and on Deansway, while inhumation burials (generally a later practice) are known from Deansway, Blackfriars and Farrier Street.

The impression of the second- and third-century settlement is of a bustling industrial town and trading centre—analogous perhaps to a settlement on the Mississippi in the early 19th century—with extensive suburbs spreading loosely along the main axial road on the river terrace down into the river margins, but with no apparent sister settlement on the west bank. With close links to the salt-producing centre at Droitwich and to the Malvern potteries (producing their distinctive orange-coloured Severn Valley Ware), and with a rich agricultural hinterland (the structure of which is still visible in the area south of Droitwich) the town would have been an important redistribution centre for local products, and it is this historic function which is likely to have been the reason for the settlement's survival—rather than abandonment—during subsequent periods of economic and social instability.

The third century seems to mark the limit of the settlement's expansion; by this point it extended over an area greater than that of the later medieval city, and during the late third and fourth centuries the effects of rampant inflation, the breakdown in continental trade and the fragmentation of administrative control which characterise this period conspired to produce a general decline in the urban population. The settlement appears to have contracted into a defended enclosure at the southern end of the river terrace (built along the line of the old Iron-Age enclosure), and the population was once again engaged with a predominantly agrarian economy. Iron production stopped during the first half of the fourth century, by which time part of the old workings along Deansway had been turned into a cemetery (containing at least fourteen burials). Archaeological evidence indicates that rubbish was being tipped in areas where previously there had been neatly laid out streets, and the Sidbury suburb had to be abandoned due to flooding caused by the silting up of the Diglis basin.

While no inscriptions or other texts can be directly attributed to the Roman settlement, the listing of towns contained in the seventh-century Ravenna Cosmography makes reference to a place called Vertis—'a place on a sharp bend in a stream or river'— which might just be Roman Worcester.

The Post-Roman Settlement, Fourth Century A.D. - A.D. 680

Although the fourth-century picture is one of a settlement steeling itself against an increasingly hostile political and economic climate, it is possible that the seeds of Worcester's later importance were sown during this period. A Roman bronze *chi-rho* (cross) found during the construction of the Lychgate centre, and the Roman nature of the dedication of St Helen's Church in Fish Street (lying just within the northern bounds of the late Roman and post-Roman defences), have been used to suggest that a Christian community developed and prospered within the area of the late Roman settlement. While more evidence is required to substantiate this hypothesis, recent studies have shown that a British Christian community, controlling a large part of what later became north Worcestershire, was probably well established on the site before the Anglo-Saxon minster church of St Peter was founded in 680. Over and above the historical evidence for this, which is primarily based on the origins and extent of St Helen's and its rural parish, the absence of pagan Saxon burials and settlement evidence from the west bank of the Severn, and from the Worcester area generally, is unlikely to have been due to natural barriers alone. Rather than being abandoned therefore, we can envisage a fifth- and sixth-century settlement whose rulers, possibly minor British kings (and possibly Christian), managed to establish control over, and defend, a large and prosperous rural hinterland until the seventh century when the area was annexed as part of the kingdom of the Hwicce.

The fifth- and sixth-century community would probably have inhabited the same defended enclosure as that occupied during the fourth century—between Copenhagen Street/Pump Street in the north, and the southern end of the river terrace—and in all probability comprised the descendants of the Romano-British population. At least one church, St Helen's, was established in the northern part of the defended area (the adjacent church of St Alban's, on Little Fish Street, may have been another), providing pastoral care to a large rural parish which in 1113 still comprised churches at Wick, Martley, Wichenford, Kenswick, Little Witley and Holt on the west bank, and Claines (Northwick), Hindlip, Warndon, Whittington, Churchill and Huddington on the east bank. While little concrete archaeological evidence is available for this period, two Christian burials found beneath the refectory undercroft (now College Hall) in the Cathedral Close may have been part of this community, while soil studies on sites on Deansway—outside the defences—have shown that the area was used as grazing land.

The Origins of the Saxon Town, 680-890, Weogornaceaster

In about 628, in a move to create a buffer zone between Mercia and Wessex, King Penda of Mercia amalgamated several small Anglian and Saxon kingdoms in the lower Severn Valley into a single political unit under the control of the Hwicce, whose territory centred on Winchcombe in Gloucestershire. Worcester fell within this territory and in 680, as part of a general reorganisation of the English church which later became the model for the secular state, Archbishop Theodore created the see of Worcester. The fact that Worcester was chosen as the see for the new diocese (covering land in modern Worcestershire, Gloucestershire and Warwickshire) is extremely significant since both Gloucester (for its size) and Winchcombe (as the Hwiccian royal family seat) might have made more suitable candidates. The choice of Worcester supports the contention that there was a well-established, and powerful, British Christian community living on the site when the area fell under Hwiccian control.

Bosel, the first Anglo-Saxon Bishop of Worcester, established his minster church of St Peter (possibly a stone building) somewhere on or near the site of the present cathedral, within the defended earthworks which had enclosed the late Roman and post-Roman settlement—an area of approximately eight hectares (20 acres). While there is no archaeological evidence for structures outside the earthwork defences until the later part of the ninth century, it is clear that the old Roman roads and streets, and probably the bridge, were still in use during this period. The silting up of the Diglis basin, which began in late Roman times, would have rendered this area unusable as a major harbour, and it was probably in this period that the foreshore on the east bank became commercially valuable for mooring and storage purposes.

A clear indication of the settlement's religious importance at this time, and the size of the rural parish its clerics served, is the possible appearance by *c.*721 of two further churches nestling within the northern bound of the defended area—St Alban's, certainly, on Little Fish Street, and St Margaret's, maybe, whose existence somewhere in the area of Warmstry Slip has only recently been identified. This large ecclesiastical community would have provided the focus around which the settlement developed in the eighth and ninth centuries, with the lay population primarily engaged with activities serving the church. As the church and its increasingly extensive rural estates prospered, so the lay community would have benefited, and the rôle of the church in stimulating and supporting commercial activity at this time cannot be overstated. An example of the bishops' economic wealth is shown by a charter of *c.*840 which documents the sale of rights over five places in the West Midlands to Bishop Heaberht by King Berhtwulf of Mercia for six horses, a gold ring, a dish, two drinking horns and three drinking vessels—the dish alone, probably silver, weighed 11 pounds. This wealth would have been underpinned by the agricultural produce and raw materials generated by their estates—for example a charter of *c.*716 records the church of Worcester holding property in Droitwich which included six salt furnaces—with an additional and considerable income from trade and commerce. Various eighth- and ninth-century charters record the bishops' extensive dealings in London, including one *c.*743 which freed Bishop Mildred from paying tolls to King Aethelbald of Mercia on two ships.

This period provides us with the earliest surviving Old English name for Worcester—Weogornaceaster or Weogernaceaster (691)—with latinised versions such as Weogorna civitas (691) and castra Weogernensis (736-7) also in use at this time.

The Saxon burh, 890-1066

Dated to between 884 and 901, Worcester's most famous Saxon charter records:

> At the request of Bishop Waerfirth, their friend, Ealdorman Ethelred and Aethelflaed ordered the borough of Worcester to be built for the protection of all the people ... and they now make it known, with the witness of God, in this Charter, that they will grant to god and St Peter, and to the Lord of that Church, half of all the rights which belong to their lordship whether in the market or the street, both within the fortifications and outside ... except that the wagon-shilling and load-penny at Droitwich go to the King as they have always done. Otherwise, land-rent, the fine for fighting, or theft, or dishonest trading, and the contribution to the borough wall and all the (fines for) offences which admit compensation, are to belong half to the Lord of the Church.

Establishing Worcester as a fortified burh, this charter marks a significant turning point in the history and urban form of the settlement, establishing the structure around which the later medieval town developed and prospered—a structure which is still visible in today's street plan. While the references to a market, trade and an urban population demonstrate that by this time the essentially religious settlement of the seventh and eighth centuries had developed many of the characteristics and problems of an urban centre (note the reference to fighting), the construction of the burh provided the opportunity for the Bishop of Worcester to regularise his powers over the lay population, and his holdings within the settlement—while of course conforming to King Alfred's policy of fortification against the Danes (the border with Danish held territory, the Danelaw, established in 886, ran along Watling Street between Chester and London).

The defences constructed by Bishop Waerfirth extended between the south side of Broad Street, in the north, and the southern end of the river terrace, and probably incorporated the southern flank of the settlement's existing earthwork defences in this area. While the line of the defences on the eastern flank of the town is uncertain, it probably ran east along St Swithin's Street before turning south between the present New Street/Friar Street alignment and the line of the later medieval city wall. The defences enclosed an area of approximately sixteen hectares (40 acres) and would have comprised a timber and stone revetted earth bank with a steep-sided ditch outside. The bridge, between Newport Street and Tybridge Street, lay outside the burh, although there may have been another (now lost), or at least a ford, within it. While the old Roman roads to Droitwich (through Lowesmoor) and Gloucester/London (through Sidbury) were still in use at this time, with the Sidbury road at least having an entrance into the south-eastern flank of the burh, the main axial road along which the Roman town had developed was abandoned in favour of the present High Street/Foregate Street/Tything alignment (which may itself have been a surviving part of the Roman settlement's street system)—indicating both the scale of the works and their significance in influencing the layout of the later medieval town.

Analysis of Worcester's reconstructed late medieval plan (illustration 1) indicates that the internal layout of the settlement initially comprised two rectangular blocks of land either side of the High Street—extending from the northern line of the old sixth- and seventh-century defences (Pump Street/Copenhagen Street), which were probably levelled during this period, up towards the northern wall of the new burh (to Bank Street/St Swithin's Street). These blocks, initially divided into four plots either side of the street (which would have been much broader than that of today), would have contained a thriving market place—although the early town would have looked more like a village, with cattle and other goods brought in from farms and estates being kept in large open plots which contained a low density of buildings. As the settlement prospered these large plots were sub-divided, with development spreading southwards to link up with the Cathedral Close (over the earlier settlement defences), westwards towards Birdport (now part of Deansway) and the river, and eastwards up to the line of the burh defences. While archaeological evidence for this period is slight, evidence for bone- and horn-working and lime-burning has been found along Deansway, while a corn-drier was discovered outside the defences at Blackfriars. Pottery was being traded in the city from as far away as Stafford and Stamford, and a lead striking of a silver coin of King Aethelred (c.991-7), found on the line of the old main Roman road at Blackfriars (which by this time had been relegated to a muddy track) may have been a discarded token used to pay tolls.

In 904, in return for their earlier favours, Bishop Waerfirth gave Aethelred and Aethelflaed a parcel of land, a haga, in the north-western part of the town, on the river between Copenhagen Street, All Saints' Church, and present-day Deansway. While the haga may have contained a royal residence, the value of the land lay in its waterfront (for trade and warehousing), although it also occupied a strategic position on the burh's north-western gateway (at the present juncture of Bridge Street, Broad Street and Deansway) to which All Saints' may have been the gate-church—note that the central part of present-day Deansway was originally called Birdport, previously Bridport Strete whose derivation might be 'the gate of the Britons'. This gate overlooked the approach roads to the river-crossing as well as a market place which survived, as All Hallows, until the time of Henry VII (1485-1509) when it was moved to Angel Place (the area was still referred to as the Beast Market, however, throughout the 18th century).

As the population of the town increased, assessed at 1,200 hides in the 10th-century Burghal Hideage (1 hide = 1 man) and probably approximately 2,000 by the time of the Norman Conquest, so did the number of churches. By the late 11th century, All Saints', St Andrew's (Deansway) and St Swithin's (St Swithin's Street) were all probably functioning as churches (although none of their Saxon fabric survives), in addition to the earlier established St Margaret's, St Helen's and St Alban's, while in the 960s Bishop Oswald (later St Oswald) replaced the secular priests serving the cathedral with a more formal monastic community of Benedictines for whom he built a new cathedral dedicated to Christ and St Mary. Completed by 983, this new cathedral functioned alongside St Peter's which survived as a building until the 11th century, after which nothing is heard of it. The site of St Mary's lies beneath the present cathedral, and while the building itself is no longer visible, walls in the later medieval cloisters and in the refectory undercroft are probably surviving parts of the late Saxon monastic complex.

Outside the burh walls, the church of St Martin's (Trinity Street/Cornmarket) was established just outside the gateway on the approach road from Droitwich, while in the south-eastern suburb outside the Sidbury gateway lay the churches of St Peter the Great and St Godwald (or Gudwal). While St Peter the Great survived as a church until 1976 (now part of the Royal Worcester site on King Street), St Godwald's never acquired parochial rights and in the 13th century became known as St Wulfstan's Hospital (now the Commandery Civil War centre), although Wulfstan himself had nothing to do with the establishment of this facility.

This period also sees the formalisation of the city's various holdings on the west bank, with charters witnessing the dealings of the priory's estate at Wick, and with at least five houses being owned in the area which later became the medieval suburb of St John's. The church of St Cuthbert's at Lower Wick, adjacent to the river-crossing to Great Malvern (on the present-day site of Manor Farm, Malvern Road), was probably established during this period, although the rôle of parish church was taken over by St John's in Bedwardine (in St John's) during the later medieval period and St Cuthbert's, to which St John's had originally been a cemetery chapel, was abandoned—although the building itself was incorporated into a manorial complex in the later medieval period, as a barn, and still survives on the site today.

In the rural hinterland on the east bank of the river, the Saxon bishops established their primary rural residence at Northwick (in the parish of Claines, near to the Severn, where it remained until the later medieval period when this was moved to Hartlebury Castle), while charters show dealings in estates at Battenhall (St Peter the Great's parish) and possibly also at Lyppard (St Martin's parish). At Warndon, the Church of St Nicholas was probably founded during this period (within the control of St Helen's, note, not the cathedral), and later became incorporated within the site of an important medieval manorial complex owned by the Beauchamp family (on the site of present-day Warndon Court Farm).

The picture of late Saxon Worcester is of a rich and thriving town, with a well managed rural hinterland, and an economy driven by a mixture of trade and local manufacturing supported by taxes levied on the river and road traffic passing through the settlement. Generally the town seems to have prospered despite the Viking threat; raids are recorded in the southern part of the Severn Valley in 893-4 and 917. However, writing in the 12th century, Florence of Worcester (the monk John of Worcester) tells how in 1041 the Danish King Harthacnut tried to raise taxes from the citizens of Worcester who, outraged at the prospect, murdered the tax-collector and nailed his skin to the cathedral door. In retaliation Harthacnut sent a raiding party which arrived to find the citizens of Worcester and the surrounding countryfolk had fled to Bevere Island (in the Severn near Claines) where they 'defended themselves vigorously against their enemies'. The Danish raiders sacked the town, possibly dismantling the northern part of the burh defences, and left.

By the time the Normans arrived, therefore, the foundations of the later medieval town had been firmly laid, and although their arrival heralded significant changes for the local population, the Saxon character of the settlement and its buildings probably survived well into the 13th century.

The Later Medieval Town, 11th-16th Centuries

Soon after the Norman invasion, and shortly before 1069, the newly appointed Sheriff of Worcestershire, Urse d'Abitot, built a motte and bailey castle in the area south of the cathedral, probably incorporating (if not replacing) the earlier defensive ditches which had ringed this end of the river terrace. The castle, initially probably of timber although later rebuilt in stone, annexed a large part of the monks' cemetery to form its outer bailey, something which prompted Archbishop Aldred of York to curse 'Hightest thou Urse? Have thou Godes kurs'. The land was finally returned to the monks in 1217, although the dispute between castle and priory was not ended until Henry III confirmed the priory's holding in 1232. While this was not the only property in the town and countryside acquired by the new Norman sheriff at the expense of the church, the impact of the Norman take-over on the town was significantly mitigated by the then bishop, Wulfstan (later St Wulfstan), who was held in the highest respect by both Saxons and Normans.

Wulfstan, who was appointed Bishop of Worcester in 1062, was the longest living Saxon bishop to stay in office following the Norman Conquest (he died in 1095), and having sworn allegiance to William the Conqueror he helped defend the castle and bridge at Worcester for William II during the rebellion of the Lords of the Marches (in favour of Duke Robert of Normandy). Florence of Worcester records that the rebels

> burst into the province of Worcester, declaring that they would burn the city of Worcester, plunder the church of God and St Mary ... Meanwhile the Normans, taking counsel, entreated the bishop to remove from the church to the castle, saying that his presence would give them more security if they should be in greater peril: for they loved him much.

Of course the church stood as much to lose from this rebellion as did the Norman sheriff, and this incident serves to highlight both Worcester's strategic importance and the extent of Wulfstan's political influence. While the city's later commercial success might have been guaranteed by its strategic position, there is little doubt that the prestige which accrued to the cathedral and city through Wulfstan's life and works helped Worcester become the most important ecclesiastical centre in the West Midlands during the medieval period.

Between 1084 and 1089 Wulfstan rebuilt the cathedral on the site of St Mary's, noting: 'We miserable people have destroyed the work of saints, pompously thinking we can do better; how much more eminent than us was St Oswald who built this church; how many holy men of religion have served God in it'. Wulfstan's grand Romanesque cathedral was constructed in a mixture of pale Cotswold limestone and green Highley sandstone, and was probably whitewashed inside and out (some fragments of this building still survive within the present cathedral, including part of the crypt). This building would have made an imposing sight in its strategic position on the east bank promontory, its close bounded on the north by Bishop's Street (now part of Deansway) and Lich Street (now beneath the Lychgate centre, the name referring to one of the main medieval gateways into the close), to the east by Sidbury (now Friar Street), and with the Norman castle an uneasy neighbour on the south side. As part of this project Wulfstan increased the monastic community from 12 to 50 (in 1104 this number had reached 61), most of whom would have held property (messuages) within the town to support the monastic community. Wulfstan, who was the first Bishop of Worcester to live outside the priory, may have lived within a building whose surviving pre-13th-century elements are still visible in the hall built by Bishop Giffard (1268-1302) in the north-western part of the close, which became the Bishop's Palace. This structure was later extended in the 15th century, and survives today within the shell of an early 18th-century building constructed by Bishop Hough.

While Domesday Book records only 141 holdings in the city (of which five belonged to Evesham Abbey), indicating a lay population of about 700, this is almost certainly an inaccurate summary—Droitwich had 150 holdings registered—and other documentary evidence suggests a more likely figure of about two thousand. At this time only the King, the Bishop, tenants-in-chief (for example Marcher Lords like Ralph de Toeni and Earl Roger of Shrewsbury), or important sub-tenants of rural estates, would have owned land in the city, with the Bishop being the most influential landowner. The most valuable land would have been along the High Street market area, with rental values for land generally in the city varying from 4d. to 2s. (the annual rent for one group of 88 houses being just over 2s. 1d.). By 1170 rental incomes had increased substantially, with a holding of 12 houses netting 4s. 6d.

While the city boundaries had still to be defined by a city wall during this early post-Conquest period, there is some evidence to suggest that settlement spread outside the northern line of the old Saxon defences (which were probably levelled at this time) into the area of the present Cornmarket, and northwards along Foregate Street (the northerly continuation of the High Street). By the late 12th century the churches of St Martin (Trinity Street) and St Nicholas (The Cross) had certainly become established in these areas, suggesting that their suburban parishes had already started to form at this time. A further suburb developed between Newport Street and Dolday down towards the river bridge, with the church of St Clement (founded c.1164) on the waterfront on the north side of this (the church was demolished in 1823, its present namesake now on the west bank of the river on Henwick Road). By 1268 the church of St Michael in Bedwardine had been established in the north-eastern part of the close as a cemetery chapel to the cathedral, indicating that by this time a relatively large lay community was living within it—until the 19th century, however, subject to the authority of the church not the civic administration. However, the church never took root in the town and was later demolished (the fate also of a Victorian successor, built in 1842, the existence of which is now marked only by the gravestones of its churchyard).

The 12th and 13th centuries proved to be turbulent times for the city, and aside from numerous accidental fires (in 1113, 1189, 1202 and 1299), significant havoc was wrought by the various rebellious and loyalist armies of the time trying to secure and hold the strategic river-crossing at Worcester. In 1139, during the civil war between King Stephen and Matilda (Henry I's only legitimate heir), the castle held out against Matilda's supporters, while King Stephen captured and burnt the city in 1150—but failed to capture the castle! In 1151 King Stephen attacked the castle again, building two temporary forts overlooking the road to Leominster and Bewdley (between Henwick Road and the river, which cuts sharply into the west bank in this location) and the London/Oxford Road, at Red Hill. This attempt failed, although the next year the castle fell into the hands of Stephen's supposed ally, the Earl of Hereford, who in fact did a deal with William Beauchamp (Urse's descendant and the castle's constable) to acquire the castle without a fight. In 1155 Worcester castle was re-fortified by Hugh Mortimer against Henry II, while in 1216 (during the reign of King John) Worcester declared for the French Dauphin, Louis, under William Marshall, son of the Earl of Pembroke. The city was taken by way of the castle, which was 'not faithfully watched everywhere', and King John gave control of the castle to John Marshall to guard against the French threat—although Henry III later threatened to pull down the city walls unless the citizens paid £100 fine for their insurrection. On his death in 1216, King John was buried in Worcester Cathedral, and it was probably on his father's wishes that Henry III ordered the northern part of the castle bailey—which had been annexed by Urse d'Abitot in 1069—to be given back to the priory.

Following the partition of the outer bailey, and the move of the Beauchamp family residence to Elmley Castle, Worcester castle's strategic military significance waned, and by 1221 it had become the King's prison. By 1263, during the Baron's War, the castle had become a weak spot in the city's defences, providing the rebel Earl of Derby with an easy entry to take the town—although both were retaken by Prince Edward in 1265. By 1459 the gaol had fallen into serious disrepair, with stone being taken from it to repair the city walls, and by 1540 it was observed that 'the castle ... is now clene downe ... The dungeon hill of the castle is a greate thinge overgrowne at this time with brush wood'. While the castle mound was refortified during the Civil War, the site returned to being a gaol until 1814 when the prisoners were transferred to the new county prison on Castle Street. The Dean and Chapter finally acquired the site in 1823, and the gaol was demolished in 1826. Between 1826 and 1846 the site was quarried for sand and gravel, bringing to light many Roman and prehistoric artefacts which give a glimpse of what important remains may have survived there buried by the Saxon and Norman earthworks—the site today lies within the grounds of the King's School.

While documentary evidence for Worcester's medieval city defences is patchy, it is clear that the town wall and ditch were complete by the first quarter of the 13th century (during King John's reign) enclosing, with the castle, an area of about thirty-three hectares (83 acres)—see Figs. 7 and 9. The wall was constructed of red sandstone (with some green) from the quarries at Holt and Ombersley, with a chamfered plinth at the base of the wall lining a steep-sided ditch, on the eastern flank, and with a fighting platform on the inside. While work on the wall probably started during the 12th century, the nature of the references suggests either that the circuit was not complete at this time, or that it kept being destroyed. The wall, whose features can be seen quite clearly on Speed's map of 1610 (illustrations 4, see also 1) ran from the

Bar Gate at the bridge—with St Clement's Gate to the north providing access to the east bank of the Severn and Pitchcroft Meadow—along the south side of The Butts (where it is still visible) to the Foregate (North Gate) on Foregate Street (demolished in 1702). From the Foregate the wall ran along the south side of Sansome Street, curving round to the east and then south along Queen Street, where the postern Trinity Gate provided alternative access from the city into Lowesmoor. From here the wall ran across the Cornmarket to St Martin's Gate (demolished in 1787), and thereon southwards to the bridge across Frog Brook which became the Sidbury Gate (demolished by the early 19th century). At this point, the natural course of Frog Brook was altered to run into the outer ditch of the castle defences, which ran along the line of present-day Severn Street (Frog Lane as was), with the Frog Gate providing access to the marshy land adjacent to the Severn on the north side of the Diglis basin, and to a mill which is recorded in this location. The cathedral had its own Water Gate, or Priory Gate, leading to the river, and radar survey has shown that a slip led up from this into the close, providing a private mooring facility for the Bishop and Prior. In 1226 the Greyfriars living on Friar Street were given permission to build a postern gate in the wall, known as Friars Gate, to allow them to collect firewood, although this had disappeared by 1820 when Union Street was built.

While there are references to five towers on the medieval city wall in 16th-century documents, only part of one still survives (the bastion at St Martin's Gate), and the location of the others is unknown. Although a Leominster Tower is recorded as being somewhere between St Clement's Gate and the Foregate, and Speed's map provides us with several possible locations for this, the destruction caused in this area during the Civil War has probably removed all surviving evidence for the feature. Within the city walls the street network of the Saxon burh, which itself had incorporated old Roman alignments, was consolidated into the pattern shown in illustration 2. As the city became more prosperous, and demand for land within its walls increased, the relatively large and open plots which had characterised the earlier medieval town were subdivided, providing greater rental incomes to the landowners and beginning a process which led to the network of properties evident for the later medieval city (see illustration 1). It was within these later, narrower plots that the densely packed timber-framed buildings most commonly associated with the medieval city developed, and evidence is gradually accruing to suggest that many of these in the town centre (primarily either side of the High Street) replaced large stone, or stone-founded, buildings which had been built at the back of the larger 12th- and 13th-century plots—away from the hustle and bustle of the street frontages.

During this time the cathedral underwent a number of changes. Following the collapse of the tower in 1175 this and the two western bays of Wulfstan's structure were rebuilt. Work was completed in 1218, when the body of St Wulfstan was translated into a shrine. Possibly to encourage pilgrimages to the relics of St Oswald, Bishop William of Blois initiated a complete rebuild of the east end of the cathedral in 1224 (completed c.1250). During the 14th century a further phase of building included: the north arcade of the nave and the north aisle, which were rebuilt c.1317-20; the Guesten Hall, which was built by Bishop Braunston in 1320 (demolished in 1862, the roof is now in the Avoncroft Museum of Buildings near Bromsgrove); the Edgar Tower gateway, which was completed in 1368-9; the refectory and cloister, which were rebuilt (on the Norman footings) in 1372; the tower, which was rebuilt c.1374; the Water Gate, which was built in 1378; and the North Porch, which was built in 1386.

During the 13th and 14th centuries the city's suburbs spread out along Foregate Street and The Tything, extending down almost to Barbourne Brook by the end of the Middle Ages, while the suburbs at Lowesmoor and Sidbury similarly flourished. The suburb of St John's developed around St John's Church, spreading down along a man-made causeway towards the bridge—which may have been a timber construction, though on stone and iron slag piers, until c.1313-28 when it was rebuilt in stone.

By this time, in addition to the cathedral, 11 churches and the Benedictine monastery, the city had acquired communities of Greyfriars (Franciscans) in c.1226 (living on Sidbury—more recently called Friar Street—although the building known as Greyfriars is a 15th-century townhouse which is unlikely to have been part of the friary complex), Blackfriars (Dominicans) in c.1347 (at Blackfriars, off Angel Lane and Broad Street—the area of the present Friary Mall), and Whiteladies (Cistercian nuns) c.1225, whose Whitstones Priory lay on the site of the present Royal Grammar School in the Upper Tything. In addition, hospitals developed along the Upper Tything at St Oswald's (later becoming almshouses which are still in use today) and at Sidbury, where St Wulfstan's Hospital (now the Commandery) lay just outside the Sidbury gateway. These institutions were mainly built in red sandstone (with some green), and following Henry VIII's Dissolution of the monastic orders many of them were demolished for their building stone, although the footings still survive in places.

As with many other medieval cities, Worcester had a Jewish population active in trade and commerce during the 12th and 13th centuries, and there is some evidence that there may have been a Jewish quarter in the area of Cooken or Coken Street (now Copenhagen Street), in St Andrew's parish, although this completely disappeared following the Expulsion of 1290.

In 1189 Worcester was granted a degree of independence from the rule of the Sheriffs (the Beauchamp family) when Richard I freed the city from the interference of the Shire administration in its financial affairs—for which a fee would have been paid both to the King and his officials. These freedoms were further extended by Henry III, who excluded the Sheriff from the legal affairs of the borough and granted the city a merchant guild. This was particularly significant since it meant that no foreign merchant could trade within the city, or its suburbs, without the permission of the burgesses, providing them with a significant amount of power and income generation from tolls and other taxes. This was not a complete stranglehold, however, and toll-avoidance was as much an issue for the authorities then as tax-avoidance is today—for example tolls on Droitwich salt were avoided by transporting it to the river by way of Castle Street (Salt Lane as was). The medieval Guildhall, a timber construction, lay on the site of the present building on the High Street (built between 1721 and 1727), and here the courts and meetings of the burgesses were held, as were plays and social gatherings. Responsibility for maintaining the city walls and bridge fell on the Guild of the Holy Trinity which was founded in 1371. It was also responsible for almshouses located in Trinity Street, although this institution came to an end following the Dissolution.

By 1377 the population of Worcester had grown to approximately three thousand, and during the 16th century this figure reached about eight thousand. This community was engaged with an enormous variety of trades and crafts (over forty are documented for the city in the late 13th century) as one might expect from a thriving medieval city, and archaeological evidence has revealed evidence for some of these including bronze-working, bell-founding, tile-making (using the locally available clays), tanning, butchering, fishing, bone-working, needle-making and minting (although only by way of the coins themselves). The success of Worcester's trading community is shown by the distances over which it did business, buying wool in Herefordshire and selling cloth in London, importing wine from south-western France, pottery from Germany and Spain, dried cod from Iceland (via Bristol), metals from the Low Countries and the Forest of Dean, and dyestuffs from the continent. The bustling waterfront quays on the east bank provided employment for boatmen and carriers, while the dense cluster of buildings which grew up from the waterfront spreading up towards present-day Deansway contained numerous inns, and The Tything became famous for its prostitutes. The rural estates around Worcester would have supplied the city with much of its basic foodstuffs, and the surviving medieval fishpond complex at Middle Battenhall Farm provides us with an idea as to the scale and sophistication of estate management at the time.

Large-scale cloth manufacture came to dominate the city's economy during the 15th century, with the Dolday/Newport Street suburb becoming the centre of the industry, and with the establishment of the Worcester Clothiers' Company, or Guild, which retained close links with the Blackfriars. By the 16th century half the employed population worked in Worcester's clothing industry as spinners, weavers, dyers, fullers and carders, and documents record famous clothiers like William Mucklow selling high-quality Worcester cloth to merchants from Brussels and Antwerp.

By the end of the Middle Ages, and thanks in part to the political and financial skills of the bishops, Worcester had become established as a prosperous regional market and religious centre, the largest town in a 20-mile radius, and with an international reputation for its products. The population by this time lived primarily within timber buildings, the few survivals including Tudor House and Nos. 14-20 Friar Street, *The Golden Lion* on the High Street, and Queen Elizabeth House on Trinity Street. While a prosperous city, the lives of many of the inhabitants would have been subject to a poverty and brutality of existence which would come as a shock today. It is therefore worth remembering that the price of Worcester's medieval greatness was paid as much by the toil and suffering of its ordinary citizens as it was by the commercial acumen of its entrepreneurs and ecclesiastical grandees.

Worcester the 'Faithful City'- the 17th Century

By the time of the Civil War, Worcester would have looked much as it did at the time of Queen Elizabeth I's visit in 1575, the city's extent shown by Speed's plan of 1610 (illustration 4). By this time a significant amount of income was being earned from taxing river-borne trade, particularly coal from Shropshire (at the highest rate in the country), although the increasing economic importance of other towns in the Severn Valley had begun to erode Worcester's regional dominance as a redistribution centre for raw materials and manufactured goods—the Severn being the second busiest European river after the Meuse during this period. The port of Tewkesbury became the main embarking point for sea-going vessels bound for Bristol and the Severn Estuary and, while the extensive road network on both the east and the west bank provided access to all the key towns and production centres in the West Midlands and Welsh Marches, the volume of taxable traffic passing through the city from these places declined.

While the clothing industry was also starting to decline during this period, with increasing competition from places like Kidderminster, it still represented the city's major employer. It is perhaps significant that both city members of the Long Parliament had made their money as clothiers and, like other manufacturing centres, Worcester's politics in the Civil War were heavily influenced by a Protestant merchant class sympathetic to Parliament—with most of the local land-holding gentry supporting the Royalist, Catholic cause. Possibly as part of a policy to pacify the increasingly hostile merchant classes, James I had enhanced the city's independence in 1628 by entrusting its government to a mayor, aldermen, a sheriff, two chamberlains, and bodies known as the 24 and the 48—the forerunner of the present civic administration. One of the first actions of this new administration, no doubt to the chagrin of James I, was to invite radical puritan preachers into the city who found particular favour with the weavers and other clothing workers whose industry was generally being threatened by the Royalists.

Adding to the impending gloom of the years prior to the outbreak of hostilities, plague hit the city in 1637 and killed as many as one in 10 of the population. When fighting did break out, Worcester once again became the focus for manoeuvring armies and political intrigue, although this time, most famously, it was site of the first and last engagements of the Civil War. The first, in the meadows at Lower Wick north-east of the medieval bridge at Powick, occurred on 24 September 1642 when a Royalist cavalry force under Prince Rupert, while retreating from the city, defeated a detachment of the Earl of Essex's Parliamentary troops under Colonel Sandys. The Parliamentary forces briefly occupied the city, defiling the cathedral, before leaving on 19 October to confront Charles I at Edgehill on 22 October. Following Charles's victory at Edgehill, Worcester became a Royalist garrison and the King visited the city twice in June 1644. Following Charles's defeat at Naseby on 14 June 1645 he considered using Worcester as his rallying point, although he finally gave himself up to the Scots at Newcastle in April 1646, leaving Worcester besieged until 22 July when the city finally surrendered. This loyalty to the Royalist cause prompted the city's later claim to be the *civitas fidelis* (faithful city), although Malcolm Atkin's recently published work on the Civil War in Worcestershire shows that the citizens were in fact extremely indifferent, and frequently hostile, to both factions—perhaps not surprising as they watched their city and livelihoods being torn apart by Parliamentary and Royalist forces alike.

During the 1646 siege Worcester's medieval walls were repaired, with massive additional earthworks in front of and behind the wall to strengthen the fragile sandstone structure against cannon fire, and the medieval suburbs were deliberately flattened to prevent the Parliamentary forces from approaching too close to the city walls. This destruction was added to by the battle of 1651, and this is the main reason why surviving medieval structures have yet to be identified in these areas—although the notable exception to this is the Commandery (at Sidbury) which managed to avoid significant damage.

On 22 August 1651, at the head of a mainly Scottish army, the Prince of Wales stopped off in Worcester to try to raise some English support and was proclaimed King (a muster was held on Pitchcroft, but this turned into a fiasco). The city defences were rebuilt, having been slighted after the 1646 siege, with a massive earthwork extending from the eastern side of the city across the Blockhouse area and Frog Brook up to Fort Royal Hill where a star-shaped fort was constructed to defend the approach road from Oxford. The Royalists, commanded by the Duke of Hamilton, had their headquarters at the Commandery (previously St Wulfstan's Hospital, but by this time the private residence of Thomas Wylde, clothier). Cromwell attacked the city on 3 September from both sides of the river, and following a major engagement at Powick broke through into St John's. At about the same time the fort on Fort Royal Hill was captured and the guns turned onto the city, which quickly surrendered. Charles only just managed to escape, and after staying in many of the county's later inns and pubs—or so we are now expected to believe—finally fled to France.

Following the collapse of Cromwell's Protectorate in 1659-60, and sensing that a peaceful restoration of the monarchy was feasible, the city and county gentry were the first to declare in favour of national reconciliation and civil peace. For the 'faithful city', it was time to get back to business. While the Civil War would have undoubtedly had a major impact on the city's manufacturers and traders—and certainly required a major rebuilding of the suburbs and repair to the cathedral—the late 17th century saw the city flourish, with a population in 1678 of about ten thousand, with its own newspaper in 1690 (*Berrows Journal*, which is still running today), and with a growing number of schools for both rich and poor (the Blue Coat School in Silver Street was founded in 1626 for 'ten poor male children aged 4 to 12'). Furthermore, the Restoration heralded a new form of urban social life developing around inns and coffee houses which littered the city centre at this time.

The Modern City

During the 18th and early 19th centuries a number of factors conspired to undermine Worcester's economic fortunes, and although the city appeared to prosper during this time—the population having risen to 20,000 by 1821—the undoubtedly splendid trappings of its most wealthy citizens, either local families or newcomers attracted by the 18th-century spa, masked an underlying economic problem whose victims, the urban poor, can be seen quite clearly amongst the more genteel images contained in this book and others like it. The growing economic importance of its neighbours (particularly Kidderminster, Stourport, Bridgnorth and the area around Coalbrookdale) led to a reduction in the volume of goods being shipped from and through Worcester, and this prompted the development of alternative routes across the Severn from both sides of the river. All the while the local landed gentry and merchants, together with a growing professional class of lawyers, doctors and financiers, were able to thrive in an economy where money could be made as easily outside the city as it could within it. Thus local investment during the 18th and early 19th centuries was concerned primarily with constructing large mansions (for example the 18th-century Blanquettes and Perdiswell Halls either side of Barbourne Brook—now demolished), grand town houses (of which the buildings in Britannia Square and at Lark Hill are fine surviving examples) and in restoring the city's churches, rather than in diversifying and developing its manufacturing base or improving the city's infrastructure.

While these projects generated work to mitigate the impact of the decline in river and waterfront employment, providing a quality of built environment that enabled it to prosper as a minor spa town during the late 18th century (a rôle taken over by Great Malvern in the 1830s with great impact on Worcester's property values), a large section of the urban population was still dependent on the clothing industry for its livelihood. It was an industry which provided but a paltry return for labour, a reflection of the stiff competition from other more favourably placed manufacturing centres. By this time Worcester had become specialised in glove-making (the Fownes factory on City Walls Road, now a hotel, being one of the few surviving buildings), the centre for this lying between present-day Deansway and the waterfront in St Andrew's parish, with the old medieval buildings here and along Newport Street and Dolday becoming the core of the urban slum which characterised the area in the late 18th, 19th and early 20th centuries. Little sign of Worcester's gloving industry remains today, however, although St Andrew's spire retains the nickname the Glover's Needle in recognition of the numerous craftsmen and their families who lived in the parish, while the poverty of the time is appropriately, though subtly, witnessed by the fact that St Alban's Church (Little Fish Street) retains nearly all of its medieval fabric—its parishioners being too poor to afford any grandification works—whereas the city's other medieval churches now exhibit predominantly 18th- and 19th-century architecture. The cathedral alone had £7,000 spent on it between 1712 and 1715, and while this heritage provides the city of today with a grand vista of church spires and architecture, it has also left an inheritance of extensive repair and maintenance bills whose size is a continuing problem for those now responsible for looking after these structures.

The poverty of the 18th-century town did not go unnoticed, however, and became an issue which the local Whig professional classes tried to address. It was in part to try to reduce local unemployment that in 1751 Dr. Wall and his 14 mainly Whig partners founded the Worcester Porcelain Works adjacent to the waterfront on Warmstry Slip (the site was later taken over by Messrs Barr, Flight & Barr), and by 1788 Robert Chamberlain, one of the many famous Worcester Porcelain painters, had set up a rival works (Chamberlain & Co.) at Diglis, on Severn Street—the site of the present Royal Worcester works (the 'royal' warrant was obtained in 1789). By the early 19th century a number of other factories had started producing porcelain in the city, most notably Grainger's at St Martin's Gate, James Hadley's on Bath Road, and the Locke works on Newtown Road.

The appointment of the pioneering Bishop Isaac Maddox to the diocese in 1743 heralded an important development for Worcester's impoverished workforce since, together with Dr. Wall, he helped form the city's first infirmary in a building on Silver Street. This building, which survives today, housed 30 patients and was one of only seven such institutions outside London at the time (the poor having been cared for by the monastic orders until Henry VIII's Dissolution). The infirmary was clearly inadequate to meet the health needs of the city's growing population and funds were raised to build a bigger facility, the Worcester General Infirmary, within its own grounds on Salt Lane (now Castle Street), which opened in 1771. It was in this hospital, which survives today as part of the Royal Infirmary Hospital, that Worcester's most distinguished physician, Sir Charles Hastings, founded what was later to become the British Medical Association. Education of the poor became a cause of the intellectuals—for varying reasons, good and bad—although the move to educate the urban population was led by the nonconformist churches, with the Congregational School in Angel Street opening in 1792, and Worcester General Sunday Schools being held in every parish by the 1830s. Work too was prescribed as a solution to the problems of the city's unemployed, and in 1702 income from the hopmarket was used to construct a workhouse on the Foregate, although by 1794 a much larger facility had been built at Tallow Hill (now demolished) and the old workhouse was turned into a warehouse and offices.

The 18th-century reconstruction of the city's suburbs which had been destroyed during the Civil War is evidenced by the numerous Georgian buildings which line Foregate Street, The Tything and Upper Tything (extending into Barbourne), while

Georgian façades can still be found on most of the buildings in the old medieval city centre (the Guildhall, built 1721-7, being the finest example) and in Sidbury, Lowesmoor and St John's. The old medieval bridge was demolished in 1781 and replaced by the present bridge which, together with the buildings along the then newly created Bridge Street, was designed by John Gwynne. A park was developed between Sansome Street, Merriman's Hill and Rainbow Hill on the eastern side of the city, which was known as Sansome Fields, later the Arboretum Gardens. Though the site was sold for development between the 1840s and '60s, areas such as Sansome Fields together with the Cherry Orchard pleasure gardens at Diglis and promenade walks in St John's and Sansome Walk provided the town's suburbs with a 'garden city' feel. Natural springs were tapped at the foot of Tallow Hill (the Spring Gardens area) and on The Butts, providing Worcester with an opportunity to exploit the 18th-century rage for 'taking the waters', while a racecourse developed on Pitchcroft—the first race was held on 27 June 1718—and the town acquired several assembly rooms (those on Shaw Street still surviving, and recently restored), bowling greens and a riding school.

The city's popularity with wealthy visitors, and its continued importance on the road network and as a regional market centre for agricultural products (in 1796 Worcester's hopmarket was described as 'the most considerable in the kingdom'), resulted in continued traffic problems during the 18th century, although this traffic also provided a significant amount of business for the town's coaching inns—primarily along Foregate Street (the *Star Hotel*) and Broad Street (the *Unicorn* and *Crown* hotels)—as well as for the occasional highwayman. Those caught were sentenced at the Guildhall until 1838, at which point the County Court was moved to the Shire Hall on Foregate Street (where it remains today) and then executed on the gibbet at Red Hill on London Road. Less serious offences, and with the many pubs and regular fairs these were regularly committed, were punishable by terms in the County Prison on Castle Street or in the City Gaol on Union Street (opened in 1824). The latter amalgamated with the county facility in 1867, and the site was later redeveloped by William Laslett for use as almshouses, which are still in use today.

It is perhaps a reflection of Worcester's underlying economic fragility that, while the city sported many of the trappings associated with the prosperity of the period, its size at the beginning of the 19th century was more or less the same as that of the later medieval town (compare illustrations 1 and 3), yet with a vastly bigger population living in increasingly squalid conditions.

Aside from the gradual decline in Worcester's manufacturing importance caused by competition from Birmingham and the Black Country, the level of the Severn itself fell significantly during the 18th and 19th centuries (possibly due to changing agricultural practices as well as the number and operation of weirs on the river) thereby reducing its usefulness for shipping generally, particularly in the stretch above Worcester. Although the economic implications of this did not go unnoticed, it was not until 1784 that plans were laid to ensure a minimum four-foot draught for boats between Worcester and Coalbrookdale. This was defeated by interests wanting a canal between Worcester and Stourport, and a later plan of 1835 to make the Severn navigable again by sea-going vessels (a 12-foot draught) up to Worcester was defeated in Parliament by a Gloucester lobby—ostensibly because of its impact on the river's salmon, but in reality to prevent Worcester from regaining its dominance as an inland port. While the construction of the weir at Diglis in 1844 helped deepen the channel down to Gloucester, the impetus and opportunity for capital investment had been captured by the railways, and it is perhaps a twist of fate, if not ironic, that there should have been so much argument over the nature of the city's rail links during the 1840s, latterly over the gauge of the track, that Worcester only acquired a rail link (and then only a narrow gauge track) in 1850 (at Shrub Hill), by which time the city had become marginalised on a line between Wolverhampton and Oxford. A line to Hereford through Malvern and Ledbury was added in 1860, and a branch line to Bromyard was opened in 1876, eventually running to Leominster.

The completion of the Birmingham and Worcester Canal in 1815 (joining the river at Diglis) provided an additional stimulus to local manufacturing, with new industries like iron founding (Hardy and Padmore, established 1814), corn milling (the Albion Mills at Diglis and the City Flour Mills at Lowesmoor), brick-making (at the foot of Lark Hill), vinegar manufacturing (Hill Evans Vinegar Works, founded in 1830, and with the largest vat in the world, holding 114,821 gallons) springing up between the Lowesmoor and Diglis canal basins in the Blockhouse area. However by this time the city's strategic position within the economy of the West Midlands had declined to such an extent that it was unable subsequently to sustain the same level of industrial development which occurred in Birmingham and the Black Country, while being too high up the Severn to benefit from the international trade coming in through Bristol. Nevertheless, what the city did produce it produced well, and the reputation of its manufactured goods during the Victorian period spread worldwide. Aside from the growing reputation of Worcester Porcelain, the Vulcan Iron Works, later McKenzie and Holland, became famous for its railway signalling equipment; J.L. Larkworthy and Co. for its agricultural equipment; and of course Lea and Perrins, whose 'Original and Genuine Worcestershire Sauce' was first made and distributed from premises on Bank Street and Broad Street before the business moved to its present site on Midland Road in 1897. Heavy engineering companies like Heenan and Froude (which moved into the city in 1903), Metal Castings (founded in 1919) and The Mining Engineering Co. (factory opened in 1925) continued this process into the 20th century, while the city's main strength developed in light engineering—exemplified by the Tower Manufacturing Co. which established works at Shrub Hill in 1890 (now based in Diglis), and by the industrial profile of the present city.

In 1826 the Government removed the import duty on foreign gloves, which essentially ended Worcester's gloving industry—one of the last industrial relics of the medieval period, although the city's links with heavy engineering can of course be traced back to the old Roman iron workings. Of the 108 manufacturers recorded for the city in 1830, only 11 were left by 1885, although boot and shoe factories were set up to make use of the population's leather-working skills (the most famous being Cinderella Shoes, founded by J.W. Willis in 1848), and other industries sprang up to fill the local unemployment gap. These included breweries at Spreckley's in Barbourne Road (founded in 1850) and at Lewis Clarke's in Angel Place (1895-1970), as well as numerous bottle factories in the South Quay and Blockhouse areas.

By the mid-19th century Worcester had developed a general educational system based on National and Parish Schools—the foundation of the modern system—although it took the city authorities 29 years before they adopted the Public Libraries Act (1850), providing a public library which was eventually located at the present site on Foregate Street in 1896 (a subscription library had previously been provided by the Presbyterian Society in Angel Place, founded in 1790). In 1833 a natural history museum was founded in Angel Street—by Sir Charles Hastings—which moved to premises on the present site of the Odeon Cinema on Foregate Street before being re-located across the road in the new library building—its current location. By the end of the 19th century the city had acquired a proper theatre (on Angel Street), with numerous pubs replacing the earlier coffee houses and coaching inns as the focal point of city centre social life—which was also sustained to a great extent by the city's agricultural markets and fairs. The northern suburb lost its Sansome Fields gardens during this period, although it gained Gheluvelt Park (at the end of Barbourne Road), while the area between the old medieval causeway on the west bank and the new link road between the bridge and St John's (New Road) was transformed from a refuse tip into Cripplegate Park in 1932 (the adjacent County Cricket Ground was established in 1897, although the county team had been playing since 1847) with Fort Royal Park—originally a private park owned by the Commandery—being given to the city in 1913.

In 1832 cholera struck the city, and while recommendations were made to improve the sanitary conditions in the city centre, the Health in Towns Society reported in 1849 that only one mile of new sewers had been laid, and that the poor were living in courts of five to 20 houses, served by one or two privies emptying into a central cesspit which itself was emptied perhaps once every six months—the worst areas lying between the High Street and the river, in the then derelict medieval suburb. Fresh water was a problem too, and in 1851 only a third of the city was supplied with this— much of the system was reliant on wells which were liable to contamination from nearby cesspits. While the 1780 Waterworks Act had prompted the construction of a pumping facility on the north of Pitchcroft to take water from the Severn to a reservoir in the Trinity (the old tower, on Tower Road, demolished in the 1960s)—later supplemented by a steam-driven pump erected on the Quay in 1807 (which continued in use until the late 1850s)—these measures were inadequate for the urban population which by then had grown to 27,000. Finally, in 1858, a new plant was built north of the old works on Pitchcroft (the core of the present Barbourne facility), pumping purified water to an 850,000-gallon-holding reservoir at Rainbow Hill (another was later built at Elbury Hill). The quality of urban life was additionally improved in 1894 when the City Council transformed the Powick Mills on the Teme, adjacent to the bridge, into a combined steam- and water-driven hydro-electric facility (an experimental design and the first of its kind). Electricity from this provided about half the city's needs, with additional power coming on line in 1902 from the Worcester Power Station on Hylton Road (by the river on the east bank). This more powerful facility soon became the city's main source of electricity, although the Powick site continued generating until the 1950s.

The late 19th century saw a gradual improvement within the urban environment, prompted in 1868 by the Artisans and Labourers' Dwellings Act which gave city corporations the powers to demolish or improve insanitary dwellings. This process was a slow one in Worcester, however, and while new housing developments sprang up for the city's workers in the outlying suburbs (at Little London, in the north of the city, for example), along the city's main roads, and beside the canal—significantly extending the size of the city by the time of the First World War—it was not until the 1920s and '30s that the old medieval slums within the city centre were cleared, thereby freeing a substantial amount of land for new development. Building of course continued for the city's more prosperous citizens, and the best surviving examples of this period can be found in Barbourne Terrace, Stephenson Terrace and along Battenhall Road.

This period of late Victorian and Edwardian expansion marks the final transition between the old medieval town and the modern city, and while this transformation and subsequent development resulted in the loss of much of the 'old' character and fabric of the place (particularly between the High Street and the river, the southern end of Friar Street and the High Street, and at Blackfriars), this might not have seemed such a bad thing to a 19th-century factory worker living in the slums on Birdport, to whom the city's medieval grandeur would in practice have been a rotting, unhygienic and hopeless environment. While these individuals may or may not have respected their heritage, they certainly had to suffer and die for it. If nothing else has really changed in the economic and geographic factors which drive the city's prosperity today (though the strategic importance of the Severn has been replaced by the M5) the population can at least enjoy the story of their city's past within a degree of comfort (at home or in one of the city's museums), without fear of disease or invading armies, and within a built environment which retains a mixture of both old and new— for everyone's benefit. While the future story of the city remains to be written, and while massive economic, social and environmental problems confront us as we approach the millennium, the citizens of Worcester today are in a better position to influence the development of their city than they have ever been—although superficially it might not seem so—and if the settlement's history has any contemporary purpose other than to record events, it is maybe to provide us with a glimpse of past mistakes and successes, so that we can truly understand the purpose and direction of our present endeavours, and those on which our futures and those of our descendants depend.

Maps and Views of Worcester

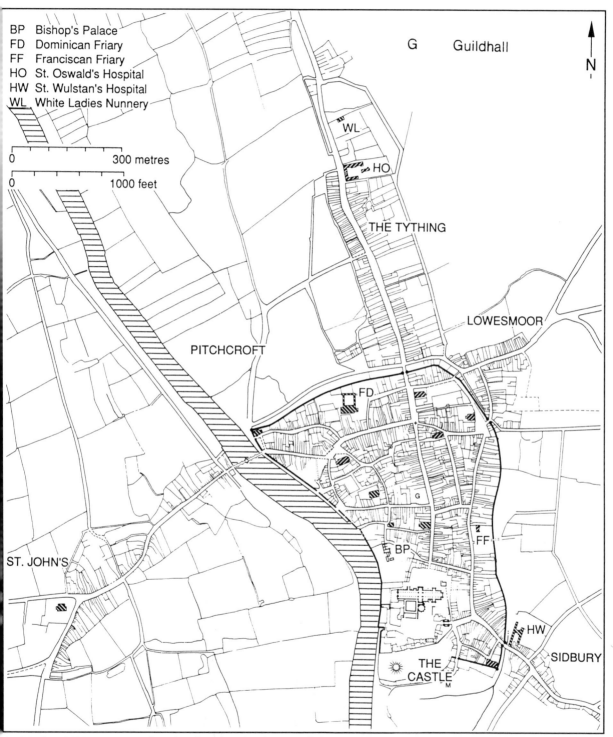

1 Medieval Worcester; a plan showing the plot layout of the later medieval town and its suburbs, with churches and other religious houses shown hatched (by Dr. N. Baker).

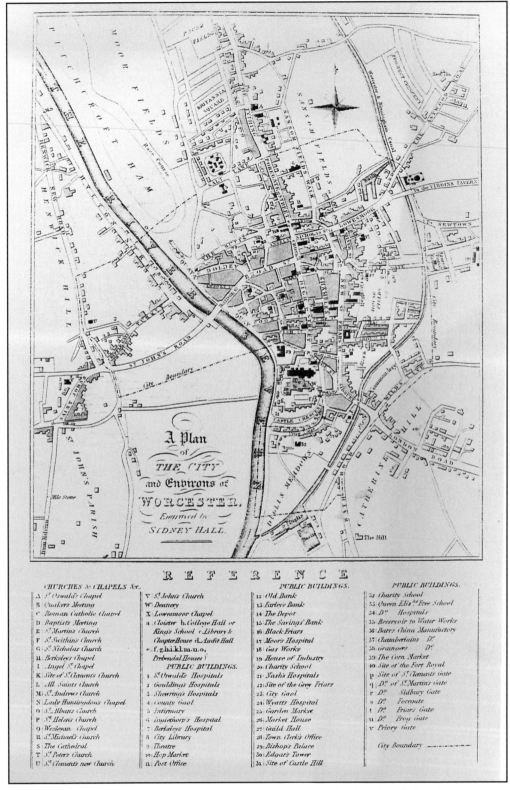

REFERENCE

CHURCHES & CHAPELS &c.

A S.t Oswald's Chapel
B Quakers Meeting
C Roman Catholic Chapel
D Baptists Meeting
E S.t Martins Church
F S.t Swithins Church
G S.t Nicholas Church
H Berkeleys Chapel
I Angel S.t Chapel
K Site of S.t Clements Church
L All Saints Church
M S.t Andrews Church
N Lady Huntingdons Chapel
O S.t Albans Church
P S.t Helens Church
Q Wesleyan Chapel
R S.t Michaels Church
S The Cathedral
T S.t Peters Church
U S.t Clements new Church

V S.t Johns Church
W Deanery
X Lowesmoor Chapel
a Cloister b.College Hall or
   Kings School c Library &
   ChapterHouse d. Audit Hall
e.f.g.h.i.k.l.m.n.o.
   Prebendal Houses

PUBLIC BUILDINGS.

1 S.t Oswalds Hospitals
2 Gouldings Hospitals
3 Shewrings Hospitals
4 County Gaol
5 Infirmary
6 Inutethorps Hospital
7 Berkeleys Hospital
8 City Library
9 Theatre
10 Hop Market
11 Post Office

PUBLIC BUILDINGS.

12 Old Bank
13 Earleys Bank
14 The Depot
15 The Savings' Bank
16 Black Friars
17 Moors Hospital
18 Gas Works
19 House of Industry
20 Charity School
21 Nashs Hospitals
22 Site of the Grey Friars
23 City Gaol
24 Wyatts Hospital
25 Garden Market
26 Market House
27 Guild Hall
28 Town Clerks Office
29 Bishops Palace
30 Edgars Tower
31 Site of Castle Hill

PUBLIC BUILDINGS.

32 Charity School
33 Queen Eliz.th Free School
34 D.o Hospitals
35 Reservoir to Water Works
36 Barrs China Manufactory
37 Chamberlains D.o
38 Grainows D.o
39 The Corn Market
40 Site of the Fort Royal
p Site of S.t Clements Gate
q D.o of S.t Martins Gate
r D.o Sidbury Gate
s D.o Forenate
t D.o Friars Gate
u D.o Frog Gate
v Priory Gate

City Boundary -----------

2 Worcester in the second quarter of the 19th century. The landmarks of the city centre are clearly shown and can be traced in the city of today. The plan pre-dates the coming of the railway in 1850, but the canal of 1815 and expanding industrial suburbs to the east of the medieval city are developed. To the north, The Tything area is becoming built up, though the streets to the north of Britannia Square are shown in their undeveloped state in the 1820s.

3 This plan of Worcester in 1816 by T. Eaton shows the city after the developments of the 18th century, when the bridge and Bridge Street were built, Foregate Street, the Infirmary and Sansome Walk were laid out, and College Street was cut through the cathedral precincts (*see also* 52). The canal is shown, but this stretch was only completed in 1815.

38   HISTORY OF WORCESTER.

REFERENCES TO THE PLAN OF WORCESTER.

PRINCIPAL STREETS.

A. Sidbury	H. Corn Market
B. High-Street	I. Mealcheapen-Street
C. Cross	K. Goose-Lane
D. Foregate-Street	L. Broad-Street
E. Tything, &c.	M. Bridge-Street
F. Friar's-Street	N. Silver-Street
G. New-Street	O. Lowesmere

CHURCHES.

a. Cathedral	g. All Saints
b. Saint Michael's	h. Saint Clement's
c. Saint Peter's	i. St. Swithin's & School
d. Saint Helen's	k. Saint Martin's
e. Saint Alban's	l. Saint Nicholas
f. Saint Andrew's	

CHAPELS.

m. Independents	p. Anabaptists
n. Lady Huntingdon's	q. Catholic
o. Presbyterian and City Library.	r. Quakers

HOSPITALS.

s. Wyatt's	w. Berkeley's
t. Nash's	x. Inglethorpe's
u. Moore's	y. Shewring's
v. Trinity	z. Saint Oswald's

PUBLIC BUILDINGS, &c.

1. Diglis Bowling-Grn.	10. Town-Hall
2. Chamberlain and Co's China Factory.	11. New Market
	12. Wilkins's Factory
3. Castle and Castle Hill	13. Reservoir
4. Commandery	14. Cold Bath
5. Priory Ferry	15 Theatre
6. Edgar's Tower, Register Office and Deanery	16 Hop-Market
	17 Infirmary
	18 Sansom-Field's Walk
7. Bishop's Palace	19 Grainger and Co's China Factory
8. Flight, Barr and Barr's China Factory.	20 New County Prison.
9. City Gaol	21 New Water Engine.

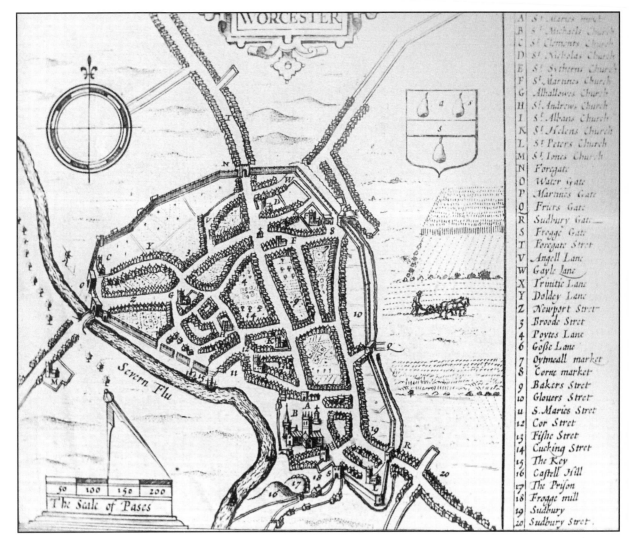

WORCESTER

A	St Maries ???
B	St Michaels Church
C	St Clements Church
D	St Nicholas Church
E	St Sythens Church
F	St Martins Church
G	Alhallowes Church
H	St Andrews Church
I	St Albans Church
K	St Helens Church
L	St Peters Church
M	St Iones Church
N	Foregate
O	Water Gate
P	Martins Gate
Q	Frurs Gate
R	Sudbury Gate
S	Frogge Gate
T	Foregate Stret
V	Angell Lane
W	Gaylt Lane
X	Trinitie Lane
Y	Doldey Lane
Z	Newport Stret
3	Broode Stret
4	Poytes Lane
6	Goße Lane
7	Oytmeall market
8	Corne market
9	Bakers Stret
10	Glouers Stret
11	S. Maries Stret
12	Cor Stret
13	Fifhe Stret
14	Cucking Stret
15	The Key
16	Caftell Hill
17	The Prison
18	Frogge mill
19	Sudbury
20	Sudbury Stret.

The Scale of Pases

Severn Flu

4 Speed's map of Worcester in 1610. This important piece of cartography shows the city largely as it appeared at the end of the medieval period. The cathedral, churches, streets, city walls and gates are clearly marked.

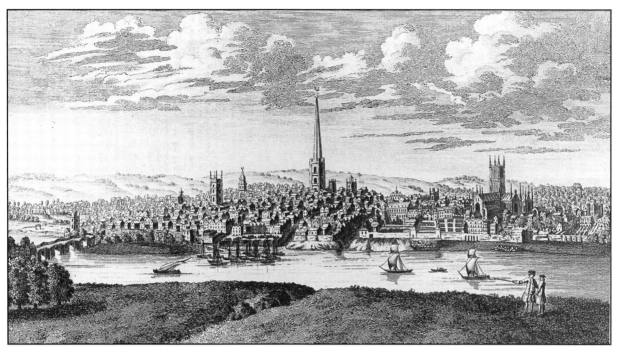

5 The city of Worcester from the west in the 1750s. The medieval bridge spans the river Severn to the north. Boats are grouped by the Quay and a trow lowers its sail to pass underneath the bridge. Inside the old walled city, the cathedral dominates the south end next to the sloping gardens of the Old Palace, and the smoking kilns of Dr. Wall's porcelain factory. Beyond rise the hills which were later to be developed as Regency and Victorian suburbs. On the extreme right the motte of Worcester Castle is visible. The motte and bailey castle was built by Urse d'Abitot, Sheriff of Worcester in 1069. During the 13th century, it ceased to be a significant military centre, though the buildings were used as a prison until 1814, when a new gaol was built in Castle Street. The motte was dismantled between 1823 and 1846.

6 Detail of an 18th-century oil painting of Worcester from the west. This section shows the cluster of church towers in the heart of the city, of which St Nicholas and All Saints are shown as rebuilt in the 1730s. By the Quay can be seen the cut, which was filled in during the construction of the new bridge and Bridge Street in the 1770s. On the right, Warmstry House is not yet developed as the porcelain works, dating the view before 1751.

7 *Above*. A riverside view of Worcester Cathedral before 1819 by Samuel Lysons.

8 *Left*. Worcester from New Road in 1828 by G. Hodson. A coach can be seen coming alongside the gardens of Cripplegate House, on the site of the Tybridge Street flats, at the St John's end of New Road. The skyline of the city centre is dominated by the spire of St Andrew's Church, which was rebuilt in 1751 by Nathaniel Wilkinson.

9 *Right*. Worcester from Hallow in 1879 by H.H. Lines. The medieval city was much rebuilt and developed in the 18th and 19th centuries. Henwick was developed as a popular suburb and place of recreation on the road to Hallow. The Portabello Tea Gardens were located here with this view across the racecourse on Pitchcroft. Before the races breakfast could be taken in the gardens.

10 Worcester from Diglis in July 1883 by S. Lines. This southern side of the city centre developed as a commercial and industrial suburb by the river and canal in the 19th century, although Diglis had been a popular place to take the air in the 18th century.

11 *Above*. A view of Worcester from Diglis after 1815, showing the canal lock and swing bridge. Diglis Meadows are now the site of Diglis Avenue and the Royal Worcester works. It has long been thought that the name Diglis is derived from the French *d'église*, but research now also suggests the Anglo-Saxon Dydda's Meadow.

12 *Left*. Worcester from the south-west across the river Severn in the early 19th century. The cathedral is surrounded by the prebendal houses of the precinct. Beyond are the Old Palace, the first porcelain factory and the churches of St Andrew and All Saints.

13 Views of Worcester from the north-east were popular in the 19th century as residential development began on the hills. Lansdowne Crescent, Rainbow Hill Terrace and Lark Hill are all evidence of Worcester's importance as a county town, as well as a commercial, industrial and social centre in the 18th and 19th centuries.

14 Worcester from the north east in 1829 showing the industrial suburbs of Blockhouse and Lowesmoor, which developed to the east of the medieval city after the construction of the canal in 1815. Nevertheless, there are still many open spaces on the city's eastern hills, including the remains of fortifications at Tamar Close and Perry Wood dating from the second battle of Worcester in 1651.

River and Bridge

15 S.S. *Worcester*, sailing alongside the South Quay, is a reminder of Worcester's important trading links via the river Severn with Europe. She made her first voyage in 1850 from Oporto, Portugal, with wines and oil cake, and traded on the Severn until 1853. There is also much archaeological evidence for Worcester's commercial connections with France and Spain in the Roman and medieval periods.

16 Since Roman times, if not before, salt was traded from Droitwich via the river Severn. Indeed Castle Street was known as Salt Lane until the 19th century. This photograph shows the Droitwich salt trow *Hastings* stuck underneath Worcester bridge during the floods of 1883.

17 The 'Great Flood' of 1886. This view of New Road on Friday 14 May shows a horse-drawn tramcar. Horse-drawn trams operated in Worcester from 1881 until electrification in 1903.

18 Long netting south of Worcester, c.1925. Salmon were fished by net from the river Severn in and around Worcester until 1929. Traditionally salmon fishermen lived in the Severn Street area and fished around Diglis weir.

19 A view of the river Severn from the cathedral taken in 1932. The scene is little different today, though many of the warehouses on South Quay and the chimney on the west bank have now gone.

20 The medieval bridge spanned the river Severn between Newport Street and Tybridge Street, and dated from at least the 13th century. The locations of earlier crossing points on the river Severn in Worcester are conjectural, but this particular site had a prominent sandbank or 'eye', which may have given its name to Newport Street, which was known as Eport Street in medieval times.

21 *Left.* John Gwynn's bridge of 1781 seen from the north in 1810. On the right are the tollhouses, whilst on the left are Gwynn's Georgian houses which stood on the corner of Bridge Street and South Quay. Bridge Street was developed by Gwynn as an area of commerce with purpose-built shops and houses. The street was completed in 1792. After years of neglect it was restored in the 1980s.

22 *Below.* Worcester bridge in 1910. Following the completion of a new bridge in 1781 to designs by John Gwynn on a site to the south of the medieval one, the old bridge was demolished. The present bridge was widened and altered in 1932.

23 *Right.* The tollhouses on the west side of Worcester bridge were painted by F. Barribal in 1931, one year before their demolition. The circular buildings were also designed by John Gwynn, and tolls were collected to maintain the bridge and New Road, which linked the bridge directly to St John's.

WORCESTER BRIDGE.

A Table of the Tolls

PAYABLE AT THESE GATES,

From and after the 30th Day of September, 1823,

Under an Act of Parliament, passed in the Fourth Year of the Reign of his Majesty, King George the Fourth, intituled "An Act for altering and enlarging the Powers of two Acts of the Ninth and Nineteenth "Years of his late Majesty, King George the Third ' for Building and completing a Bridge at Worcester "over the River Severn, and for opening convenient Avenues thereto.'"

By the Act above-mentioned, it is enacted, That from and after the 30th day of September next after the passing thereof, the several Tolls granted by the said recited Acts should cease and be no longer paid ; and that instead thereof the following Reduced Tolls shall be demanded and taken by the Collector or Collectors before any Horse, Cattle, Beast, or Carriage shall be permitted to pass the Toll Gate or Gates erected by virtue of the said Acts, (that is to say)

	£. S. D.
For every Horse, Mule, or other Beast, drawing any Coach, Berlin, Chariot, Chair, Chaise, Calash, Hearse, Litter, Caravan, or other Carriage, the Sum of	0 0 3
For every Horse, Mule, or other Beast, drawing any Waggon, Cart, Wain, or other Wheel Carriage, the Sum of	0 0 1
For every Horse, Mule, or other Beast, drawing any Sledge, Trolley, or Dray, with or without Wheels, the Sum of	0 0 1
For every Horse, Mule, Ass, or other Beast of Burden, laden or unladen, and not drawing, the Sum of	0 0 1
For every Score of Oxen, Cows, or neat Cattle, the Sum of	0 0 10
And so in proportion for any less number.	
For every Score of Calves, Swine, Sheep, or Lambs, the Sum of	0 0 5
And so in proportion for any less number.	

REGULATIONS.

Collectors, if required, to give Tickets (gratis) on receipt of any Toll.
Tolls not to be taken more than once a Day (computed from Twelve o'Clock at Night to Twelve o'Clock the succeeding Night) in respect of the same Carriages, Horses, or other Cattle, if Ticket produced denoting previous Payment.
Horses travelling for Hire, under the Post Horse Duties Act, returning without the Carriage, in respect of which Toll shall have been paid, or with the Carriage empty, or not engaged or employed on a fresh Hiring, to pass Toll Free, if returning before Nine o'Clock of the succeeding Morning.
Horses or other Beasts drawing any Stage Coach, or any Stage Waggon, Van, Caravan, or other Stage Carriage, carrying Passengers or Goods for Hire, and returning same Day, are chargeable with Toll for passing and repassing ; and Horses or other Beasts drawing any Post Chaise, or other Carriage travelling for Hire, to pay Toll every Time of passing and repassing over the same Bridge on the same Day with a Ticket denoting a fresh Hiring.
Toll Collectors may stop and prevent the passing of any Person neglecting or refusing to pay the said Tolls, or of the Horse, Beast, Cattle, Carriage, or other thing for which Tolls ought to be paid ; or may seize and detain the Goods and Chattels of such Person, or such Horse, Beast, Cattle, Carriage, or other thing, together with their respective Bridles, Saddles, Gears, or Harness (except the Bridle or Reins attached to any Horse or Beast) ; and if the Tolls, with reasonable Costs of Distress, be not paid in Four Days, may sell the Distress, rendering the Overplus on Demand to the Owner.
Toll Collectors neglecting to affix their Names on the Front of the Toll House, or demanding or taking greater or less Toll than authorised by the said Act, or from Persons exempt from Toll, or refusing to give their Name, or giving a false Name to any Person having paid the Toll, or unnecessarily detaining or wilfully obstructing any Passenger, or using any abusive or scurrilous language, are liable to a Penalty not exceeding £5, as the Justice before whom the Information shall be laid may adjudge.
Justices of the Peace authorised to hear and determine all Disputes respecting the demanding or taking of Toll, or the Amount of Toll due, or the Charges of Distress.
Penalty not exceeding £5 on Persons evading the Tolls by forged, counterfeited, or altered Tickets, or forcibly or fraudulently passing through the Gates with any Horse, Carriage, Cattle, or Beast, or taking off or putting to any Carriage, any Horse, Beast or Cattle ; or loading or unloading any Goods or Merchandize, or other things from or out of any Carriage.

EXEMPTIONS.

All Exemptions allowed by the recited Act of 19th George 3rd Repealed, and the following Exemptions are by the above Act granted, namely,
No Toll on any Horse or Carriage attending his Majesty or any of the Royal Family.
Or for any Horse, Beast, Cattle, or Carriage, Conveying, Fetching, or Guarding any Mails of Letters and Expresses, under the Authority of his Majesty's Postmasters General, or in Returning.
Or for any Soldiers upon their March, or upon Duty, or for any Horse, Beast, Cattle, or Carriage, attending them with their Arms and Baggage, or Returning after having been so employed.
Or for any Waggon, Wain, Cart, or other Carriage whatsoever, or the Horse or Horses, or other Cattle drawing the same, which shall be employed in Conveying any Ordnance, Barrack, or Commissariat, or other Public Stores, or of belonging to his Majesty, or for the use of his Majesty's Forces.
Or for any Waggon, Cart, or other Carriage, which shall be Laden only with Muck, Soil, Ashes, or other Manure for Land, or which shall be returning empty, after having been so Laden.
Or for any Coach, Berlin, Landau, Chariot, Calash, Chair, or other Carriage, or Passenger on Horseback, going to or returning from any Election of a Knight or Knights of the Shire to serve in Parliament, for the County of Worcester, on the Day or Days of such Election, or on the Day before or the Day after such Election shall begin or be concluded.
Or for any Person or Persons going to or returning from his, her, or their proper Parochial Church or Chapel.
Or from any Person or Persons going to or returning from his, her, or their usual Licensed Place of Religious Worship, Tolerated by Law, on Sundays, or any Day on which Divine Service is by authority ordered to be celebrated.
Or for any Horse, Beast, Cattle, or Carriage travelling with Vagrants sent by Legal Passes, or any Prisoner sent by any Legal Warrant, or returning after having been so employed.
Or for any Volunteers upon their March, or upon Duty, or in going to or returning from the Place of Exercise.
Or for any Horse furnished by or for, or belonging to any Corps of Yeomanry or Volunteer Cavalry, and rode by him or them, in going to or returning from the Place appointed for and on the Days of Exercise ; provided such Persons be Dressed in the Uniforms of their respective Corps, and have their Arms, Furniture, and Accoutrements, according to the Regulations provided for such Corps respectively at the time of claiming such Exemption.
Any Person claiming and Taking the Exemptions, and not being Entitled thereto, to forfeit a Penalty not exceeding £5.

ADDITIONAL TOLLS FOR OVERWEIGHT.

By the aforesaid Act, the Collectors are required and authorised to Receive, Take, and Demand (over and above the Tolls aforesaid,) the like Sums of Money as additional Tolls for Overweight, as are granted by an Act passed in the 3d year of the Reign of his present Majesty, intituled "An Act to amend the General Laws now in being, for Regulating Turnpike Roads in that part of Great Britain called England," subject to such of the Exemptions as are in that Act expressed, and also to an Exemption of any Carriage in the Service of his Majesty's Forces, carrying Ordnance, &c.

W. WELLES, Clerk to the Trustees.

24 A table of tolls at Worcester bridge from 1823.

25 A floating church for those employed on the river and canal was founded after 1816 by the Rector of St Clement's, John Davies, who became known as the Apostle of the Watermen. Davies' memorial can be seen in St Clement's Church.

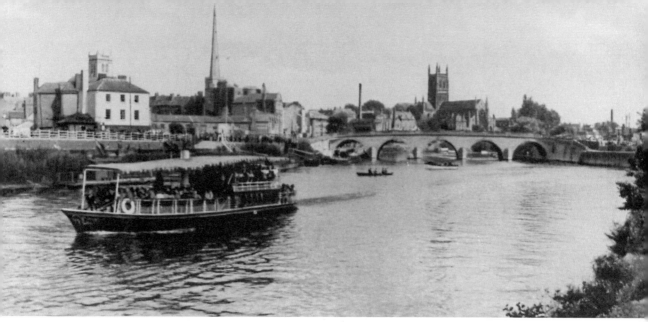

26 *Above*. A postcard from the 1930s of Worcester's most famous view. Taking a pleasure boat upstream and downstream from Worcester has been a popular outing since the 19th century. This view is little changed today.

27 *Left*. Worcester Cathedral with its 18th-century pinnacles seen from the bridge. To the left can be seen the Old Palace and the Royal Worcester Porcelain works at this date, 1804-13, of Barr, Flight & Barr. The works was founded on this site, Warmstry House, by a group of trustees led by Dr. John Wall in 1751.

28 *Right*. The construction of Diglis weir and locks in 1844 enabled transport ships of four feet draught to reach Worcester. The city was an important inland port into the 19th century, busy with steam tugs, trows and narrow boats.

29 Diglis Weir in the 1930s. Today the banks of the river are lined with trees and the factory chimneys around Diglis Basin have been demolished.

30 The confluence of the rivers Severn and Teme to the south of Worcester from a print of 1825. In the background can be seen the Malvern Hills and the tower of Powick Church. The meadows around the river Teme were the scene of much fighting in the second battle of Worcester in 1651. The sailing vessels or trows carried cargo between Worcester, Gloucester and Bristol.

The Cathedral Area

31 This view of Worcester Cathedral was taken in the early part of this century. The cathedral is sited on a piece of high ground on the opposite side of the river Severn to the flood plain, known at this point as Chapter Meadows. Now the site of the County Cricket Club and the King's School playing fields, the land was farmed as meadow land from the medieval period until this century.

32 The west end of the cathedral by the Watergate. The prebendal houses which incorporated the remains of the monastic infirmary and reredorter were demolished from 1843 onwards and the present gardens laid out. The tall pinnacles were erected in the early 18th century and were gradually removed after 1832. This view was painted by T. Pennethorne in the early 19th century.

33 *Left*. This medieval vaulted chamber was part of the monastic infirmary, which stood to the west of the cathedral church. After the Dissolution it was incorporated into a prebendal house, which in turn was demolished in 1851. This view by H.H. Lines dates from September 1873.

34 *Below*. H.H. Lines produced a series of drawings and watercolours of buildings around the cathedral before their demolition in the 19th century. This view shows the Cathedral Precincts from across the River Severn looking east. The left-hand part of the drawing was produced in 1834, but Lines added the portion below right to show houses which had been demolished by 1870. The large house to the left of the cathedral still stands as 10 College Yard. The pinnacles at the west end of the cathedral have been removed, but the west window of 1789 is shown, prior to its replacement in 1864-5.

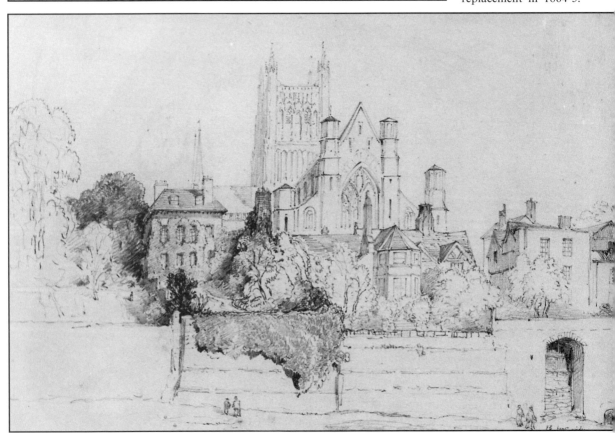

35 *Right.* The north porch of the cathedral in 1858 by W.C. Eddington. The 14th-century porch replaced a Norman structure, though the whole of the front was replaced in a restoration of 1865 by A.E. Perkins, at which point the present statues were placed in the niches.

36 *Below right.* The Water Gate, built in 1378, gave access to the monastic precinct from the river Severn. In medieval times the river was tidal, and so the gateway would flood twice a day, creating a small dock where boats could unload. A note beneath this drawing of April 1881 by H.H. Lines reads that the roadway had been raised by four feet.

37 The crypt of the cathedral was begun in 1084 and is a significant part of the building of Bishop Wulfstan. This view was painted by H.H. Lines in 1844.

38 The chapter house dates in the main from the early 12th century, although the large windows were inserted in the late 14th century. It is the earliest circular chapter house in the country, and was the daily meeting place of the chapter, where the business of the cathedral and monastery was discussed.

39 This passage led from the east walk of the cloisters to the monks' cemetery. It was built in the Norman period, but much of the masonry appears to be reused material from the Saxon monastery on the site. It was painted by H.H. Lines in 1844.

40 Between the south transept of the cathedral and the chapter house is a complex set of rooms including the monastic treasury, painted by H.H. Lines in September 1844.

41 A passage near the treasury, painted by H.H. Lines in September 1844. Several of these rooms contain medieval tile pavements.

42 The western side of the Guesten Hall, painted by H.H. Lines in 1844. The site of the hall is now a lawn to the south of the cathedral. It was demolished in 1862-6, but the fine timber roof was saved and reused in Holy Trinity Church, Shrub Hill Road. It is now on display at Avoncroft Museum of Buildings.

43 Only the eastern wall of the Guesten Hall was allowed to remain, photographed here in the late 19th century. Beyond, the Chapter House and the east end of College Hall can be seen.

44 The Deanery was adapted after the Dissolution from the Priors House, which had been built in 1225 to the east of the Guesten Hall. The house was demolished in 1845 when the Deanery moved to the Old Palace. H.H. Lines painted the kitchen in October 1844. Today only the right-hand (south) wall and windows remain.

45 The kitchen porch and the back of the Deanery before demolition in 1845. H.H. Lines painted this view in September 1844.

46 Part of the chapter house and the passage leading from the cloister to the north-west corner of the Guesten Hall, painted by H.H. Lines in October 1844.

47 College Hall from an early 19th-century print. The Norman refectory was rebuilt in the 14th century. The room has been used by the King's School since about 1560. This view facing west shows the roof and gallery prior to later 19th-century modifications.

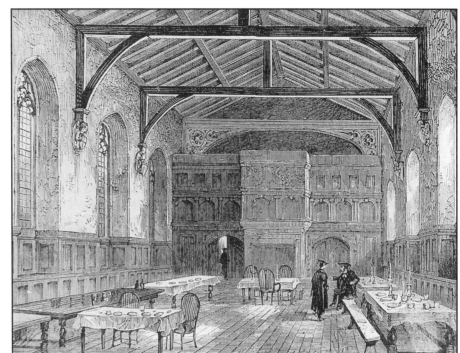

48 College Hall, looking east in the early 20th century. Beyond the platform are the damaged remains of a sculpture of Christ in Majesty surrounded by the symbols of the Evangelists. It was carved *c.*1220-30, and was reused when the refectory was rebuilt in the 14th century. The niches and friezes date from this time.

49 The prebendal houses on the south side of College Green, from an early 20th-century postcard. These are still in use by the King's School as boarding houses, but the trees and railings have long since disappeared.

50 Edgar Tower, painted in 1781 by W. Williams. This fortified gateway was built in the mid-14th century and formed the entrance to the monastic precinct. It was formerly known as St Mary's Gate. In the 18th century it was thought it had been built during the reign of King Edgar in the 10th century, and so it became known as Edgar Tower. The present statuary was added in 1912. The view offers an interesting glimpse of some of the houses in Edgar Street and College Green.

51 Old St Michael's Church in c.1800, copied from an old painting by E.A. Phipson. The church was demolished in 1842 and replaced by a new building on the north side of College Street. The site of the medieval building is marked by a group of grave memorials beside College Precincts.

Lychgate

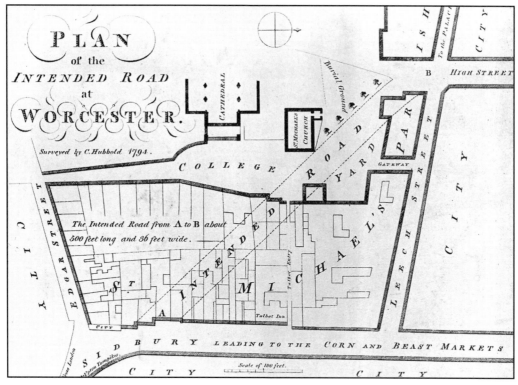

52 The great volume of traffic approaching Worcester from the south during the 18th century led to the building of a new road by the Upton Turnpike Commissioners in 1794. The road linked Sidbury to the south end of High Street, avoiding narrow Lich Street. College Street, as it was to be known, cut across the north-east corner of the Cathedral Close, breaking up the enclosed precinct.

53 St Michael's Church and the west end of College Street in February 1938 by H. Romer. St Michael's Church was rebuilt in 1839 across the road from the original site. The buildings around it formed the north side of the Cathedral Precincts, and the medieval Lich Gate stood by the church. St Michael's, the Lich Gate, and the *Punch Bowl Inn* (on the right in this view) were all demolished by 1965 when the present Lychgate Shopping Centre was built.

54   The Lich Gate by F. Barribal. The gateway gave access to the burial ground on the north side of the cathedral from Lich Street in medieval times.

55 The Lich Gate from Lich Street in 1878. The back of St Michael's Church is on the right. This timber-framed gateway was very similar to Abbot Reginald's gateway in Evesham. It was demolished in the 1950s.

56 The back of 22 Lich Street in 1902 by E.A. Phipson. The buildings of most city centre streets were on long narrow plots with a short street frontage. These burgage plots were laid out in medieval times, and allowed for each premises to have a shop front and living accommodation, with yards and workshops behind. Many of the yards were increasingly built up in Georgian and Victorian times.

57 The south side of Lich Street in 1901 by E.A. Phipson. Lich Street was a medieval thoroughfare linking High Street to Friar Street and Sidbury. It was an attractive street of timber-framed and brick buildings, but had fallen into decline by the early years of the 20th century. It was cleared in the 1950s and '60s.

58 Lich Street in 1904 by E.A. Phipson. Friar Street can be seen in the background, and on the right parts of St Michael's Church and the Lich Gate.

High Street

59 The south end of High Street in the 1930s by F. Barribal. As today, this scene is dominated by the cathedral and the large house, College Grates, which takes its name from a second medieval entrance into the Cathedral Close from the north on this site. The buildings to the left were replaced by the roundabout, and the statue of Sir Edward Elgar stands where the children are shown playing, close to the site of the Elgar family's music shop.

60 Dated October 1860, this is a general view of the southern part of High Street. A line of Georgian frontages stretches north from the cathedral to Fish Street, where the east end of St Helen's Church is seen with doorways prior to the restoration of 1879. St Helen's is now a branch of the County Record Office.

61 St Helen's Church in 1878 before restoration, when the dormer windows were removed. Much of the fabric is late medieval, though the site may have been used for worship as early as the late Roman period. The 12th-century parish extended from Martley in the west to Oddingley in the east, reflecting St Helen's rôle as a major church in Anglo-Saxon Worcester.

62 The Market Hall from Stanley's *Worcester and Malvern Guide* (*c*.1853), which states, 'Our Market Hall may now well vie with any other of its size in the Kingdom, alike for its elegance of design and adequacy of accommodation'. Built in 1804, the Market Hall stood opposite the Guildhall until it was demolished in the 1960s. The clock above the entrance was given by Richard Padmore in 1849, and can still be seen above the entrance to the City Arcade.

63 Amongst the market stalls early this century was Sigley's China, shown in this photograph of 1910. The successor to this still exists as Pratley's china shop in the Shambles. The present market hall, between the Shambles and New Street, is the former meat market.

64 & 65 The Guildhall dates from 1721-3, at which point it replaced a medieval timber-framed building. It is Worcester's principal civic building and houses the Assembly Room and the Mayor's Parlour. These unusual views show the fine Georgian frontage draped for the death of Queen Victoria on 2 February 1901 and decorated for the coronation of King George V on 22 June 1911.

Friar Street and north east to Lowesmoor

66 Friar Street, painted by E.A. Phipson at the turn of the century. This is a little known version of a very popular view, showing the 15th- and 16th-century timber-framed houses at the north end of the street. The scene is largely unchanged today, and is one of the few places where it is still possible to feel the atmosphere of the late medieval period in Worcester's streets.

67 Another view by E.A. Phipson shows the back of the Greyfriars in 1896. This large timber-framed house was built about 1470 next to the friary by a wealthy Worcester citizen. After years of being subdivided, it was restored this century by Mr. and Miss Matley Moore, and presented to the National Trust.

68 Friar Street in 1931 looking north. The railings to the right are around Laslett's Almshouses built in 1912 on the site of the City Gaol, which had been erected on the site of the Franciscan friary from which the street takes its name.

69 Number 13 Court, Friar Street, in 1903 by E.A. Phipson. The backs of these buildings still survive on the west side of the street, but many of these courts and alleys became very squalid in the 19th century and were cleared earlier this century.

70 This 19th-century illustration of old houses in New Street shows Nash House, the fine four-storey timber-framed town house which dates from the 17th century. It was then a furniture shop belonging to the Slade family. The house to the right is on the site of the home of Alderman John Nash, Mayor of Worcester in 1633. New Street is the continuation of Friar Street—'new' in that most of the properties were rebuilt in the 16th century. It still contains an attractive mixture of 16th- and 17th-century timber-framed and 18th- and 19th-century brick buildings.

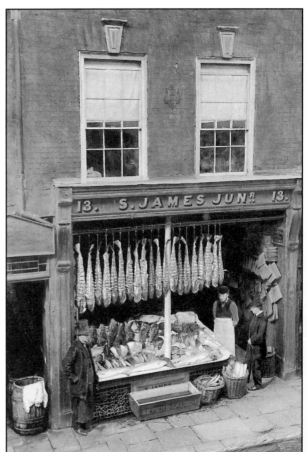

71 14-15 The Shambles in 1890 by E.A. Phipson. Few buildings of pre-1900 date survive today in The Shambles. This property with its wide timber-framed gable was a prominent feature on the west side of the street. The Shambles was largely occupied by butchers' premises from the medieval period until the 1930s.

72 13 The Shambles was James's fish shop in the early part of the 20th century, illustrated here in this unsigned painting. Many of these Georgian brick façades in The Shambles concealed medieval timber buildings.

73 Queen Elizabeth House before its re-location in 1891, by E.A. Phipson. This 15th-century galleried timber-framed building was part of the almshouses of the Trinity Hospital. The alley beneath the building is Trinity Passage, now known as the Trinity at this point. Local tradition claims that Queen Elizabeth I addressed the people of Worcester from the balcony, but she is more likely to be connected with the building through an endowment to the hospital. The present Queen Elizabeth Almshouses are situated in Upper Tything.

74 In 1891, Mayor Smith-Carrington raised money to save the building from a road improvement scheme and it was moved on greased rails to an adjacent site. This view by F. Barribal shows it much as it appears today, though the chimney has been removed. A complete exterior renovation was carried out in 1995, and the house is currently used by Worcester City Museum.

OLD TRINITY HOUSE. WORCESTER.

75 Sansome Street, looking east in August 1975 prior to road widening. St George's Roman Catholic Church dominates the view. The stone façade was added in 1887 to the brick church of 1829. That many local families retained strong Roman Catholic loyalties after the Reformation is reflected in the 1764 foundation date of a church on this site, before the Catholic Emancipation Act of 1829. Sansome Street contained many hop warehouses in the 19th century, adjacent to the Hopmarket, part of which is visible on the right.

76 The junction of Sansome Street and Lowesmoor in August 1975, with Silver Street in the background. Sansome Street was formerly known as Town Ditch, a reminder that it lay outside the medieval city walls and was developed in the 18th century on the line of the ditch. In the centre of the view is a lamp standard made from one of the supports for the tram wires. Electric trams functioned in Worcester from 1904 to 1928.

77 This undated view by E.A. Phipson shows cottages in the Trinity which were next to Queen Elizabeth House. All these buildings formed part of the Trinity Hospital, which had a hall and chapel either side of the present Bridge House in Trinity Passage. The Hospital was a medieval foundation run by the Guild of the Holy Trinity. The massive brick chimneys were a conspicuous feature of the streetscape, but were lost when the cottages were demolished in the 19th century.

78 The interior of the Music Hall in the Cornmarket as shown in Stanley's *Worcester and Malvern Guide*, *c*.1853. The building was completed in 1849 for use as a corn market, but was abandoned in favour of the Corn Exchange in Angel Street. It had become a public hall for more general use by the 1890s, but was demolished in 1966. The site is now a car park.

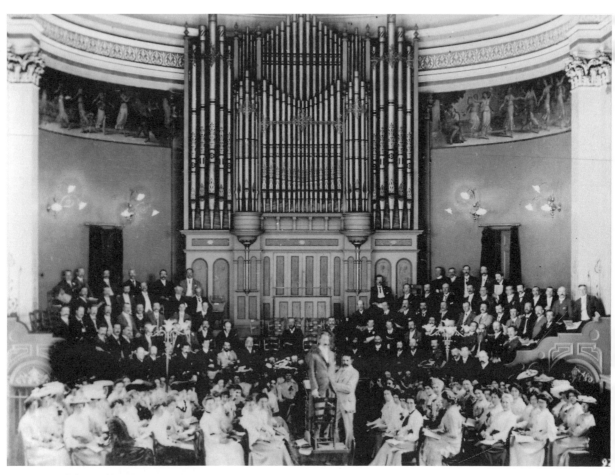

79 *Left.* The Public Hall during the 1905 Three Choirs Festival, showing Sir Edward Elgar and the Festival Chorus in front of the Nicholson organ. John Nicholson founded his organ works in 1840 near to the cathedral, and built organs for churches and halls all over the country. Production continues today from Malvern.

80 *Below left.* The open countryside of Blockhouse Fields, to the east of the city walls, became heavily built up in the 19th century with small cottages and large factories. This photograph of 1980 shows one of the last surviving Blockhouse views, which was lost with the demolition of Sigley's sweet factory (on the right) soon after. The premises of E.H. Quinton (on the left) are now absorbed into Tannery Mews, Carden Street.

81 *Below.* Fownes glove factory was specially constructed in 1884, when the company returned to Worcester and revived a declining industry. This photograph of about 1890 shows the finishing shop, where women stitched the seams of the gloves. The factory is now an hotel on the east side of the City Walls Road.

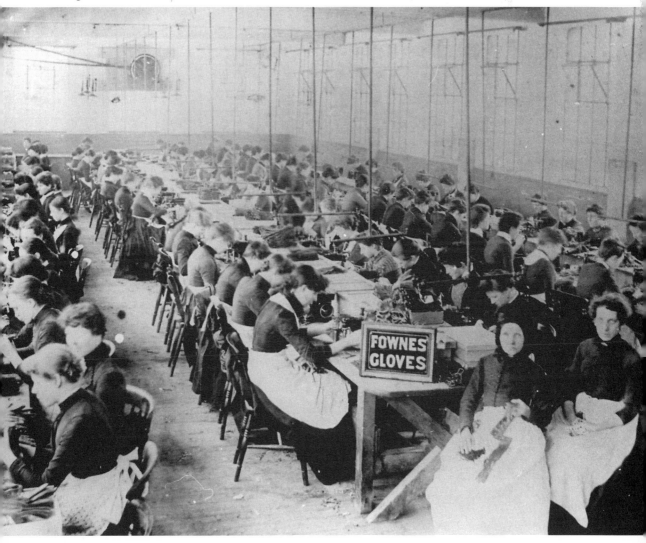

82 St Paul's Church was completed in 1887 to designs by A.E. Street. It is one of the few remaining Victorian buildings in the Blockhouse area and is well-known for its associations with the Rev. G.A. Studdert-Kennedy, or 'Woodbine Willie'. During the First World War he became famous as a chaplain for handing out Woodbine cigarettes along with bibles to troops in the trenches. These views show the interior of this church much as it would have been when Studdert-Kennedy was vicar and before substantial alterations were made in 1988 to adapt the church for current worship.

83 A little-known piece of Worcester's ecclesiastical history was lost with the demolition in *c*.1971 of St Peter's Sunday School in Lock Street, off Park Street. Built to serve a parish which had become rapidly urban in the 19th century, this small building with its Gothic iron window frames was typical of the Midlands.

84 A cottage and its occupants in Little Park Street in 1926. Many small houses which had been built during the expansion of Worcester in the 19th century were refurbished in the 1920s by the City Council. The area was finally cleared in the 1950s.

85 Lowesmoor developed as a suburb of the medieval city, along one of the main routes east from the city walls. Such suburbs were not, however, encouraged by the civic authorities, except where they provided a home for industrial activity, such as smithing or tanning. These occupations were noxious and required too much of the limited spaces within the walls. Most of the suburbs around the walls of Worcester were destroyed in the Civil War, and were rebuilt during the 18th and 19th centuries throughout the great industrial expansion. A few examples of earlier timber-framed buildings survived into the 20th century. No. 22 Lowesmoor, painted by E.A. Phipson in 1904, has since been demolished.

86 This building in Shrub Hill Road greets visitors arriving in Worcester by train at Shrub Hill station. Originally constructed as an engine works, it was adapted for use to house the Worcestershire Exhibition from July to October 1882, at which works of art and manufactured products from the county were shown.

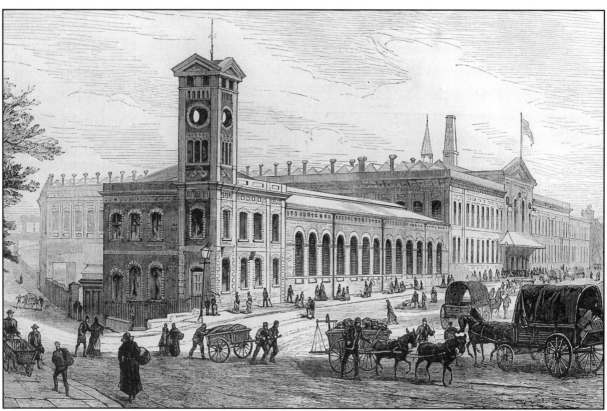

The City Walls

87 The city walls around Worcester appear to have been complete by 1216. Along with the ditch, which lay beside them, and with the river Severn and Worcester Castle, which stood on the site of the King's School, the walls fortified the city against attack. They also provided great civic status and formed a firm dividing line between the city and the surrounding country which could only be breached by a series of gates. This meant that the city's rights to charge tolls on goods and services, granted initially by Richard I in 1189, could be jealously guarded. The line of the walls can still be traced around the present city centre.

88 This view by H.H. Lines shows the walls to the south of the Watergate as they appeared in 1833. The present *Diglis Hotel* can be seen in the background and the muddy shores of the river Severn are at the foot of the sandstone masonry; the Promenade was not constructed until 1844. Below the cathedral is one of the few places where a sense of the size and importance of the medieval city walls can be experienced.

89 This 1878 sketch shows the church of Old St Martin and in the background the tower of St Swithin, beyond a small piece of sandstone walling which would appear to be part of the city walls as they ran parallel to Silver Street and Queen Street. It is a remarkable early record of the wall at this point where City Walls Road now passes.

90 *Above.* The eastern stretch of the city walls became little more than a property boundary with the development of the Blockhouse in the 19th century. After the clearance of properties in the 1970s, the wall was once again revealed, with its massive plinth of medieval sandstone blocks, the upper parts much patched with later brickwork. This view shows the City Walls Road under construction in August 1975. The remains of the wall can be seen on the left, with the backs of property in New Street and the Cornmarket beyond. The space in the centre is now occupied by the St Martin's Gate roundabout.

91 *Above right.* An aerial view in 1975 across the line of the city walls, which is behind the digger and parked cars. In the centre of the picture can be seen a long low building, formerly Wyatt's Almshouses, which has recently been extended and converted into flats. The almshouses were founded for six poor men by Edward Wyatt, Mayor in 1696. On the skyline to the left stands Townsend's flour mill in Diglis, whilst in the centre the former Cinderella shoe factory and Winwoods property is undergoing conversion to become part of Worcester's College of Technology. On the right behind the car park ramp is the east end of the cathedral.

92 *Right.* Fownes glove factory stood in Talbot Street, seen here congested with parked cars in 1975. Talbot Street was erased from the Worcester street map with the construction of City Walls Road, which the glove factory (now an hotel) fronts today. Fownes Gloves was one of the last surviving glove factories in Worcester, operating well into the 20th century. A timber-framed gable of the Commandery is visible beyond, beneath the Regency houses on Greenhill.

93 The site of the southern end of City Walls Road in 1975. The low brick wall in the centre conceals the canal, beyond which the Commandery can be seen. Above the buildings of Sidbury stands the tower of St Peter's Church, demolished in 1976.

94 A similar view, but looking across the line of the city walls towards Sidbury in 1975. The roof timbers of 59 Sidbury were exposed during restoration. Beyond the lorry can be seen the roofs of the Museum of Worcester Porcelain housed in the former St Peter's Junior School. The corrugated iron fence marks the line of the city walls.

The Sidbury Area

95 The junction of Sidbury and Edgar Street was painted in about 1930 by N. Davison. The road was widened into a dual carriageway in the 1950s, though the buildings in the background remain much the same today. Sidbury had its origins in Saxon times as the southern part of the town.

96 Behind 34 Sidbury stood these timber-framed houses in Angel Court, which took its name from the *Angel Hotel*. They were painted in 1902 by E.A. Phipson. Today the site is cleared but the gables of 34 Sidbury can still be seen from King Street car park.

97 Severn Street runs from Edgar Street to the river. It was formerly known as Frog Lane and passed out of the medieval city through Frog Gate. Today it runs between the Royal Worcester Porcelain Works and the King's School. These cottages stood on land now occupied by the school, and were painted by E.A. Phipson in 1905. Many of the houses in Severn Street were once occupied by salmon fishermen.

98 The rear of 44 Severn Street in 1935, prior to demolition. The building to the left, painted black and white, is the *Fountain Inn*, which was rebuilt and is now known as the *Potters*. In the background are the premises of Royal Worcester.

99 King Street in 1935 lined with timber-framed and brick cottages. Chamberlain's porcelain factory developed on the site behind the buildings to the left and, on amalgamation in 1840 with the factory founded by Dr. Wall, this became the Royal Worcester Porcelain Works which still flourishes on the site today.

100 *Left*. The south side of the buildings in King Street in 1935 before demolition. In the background can be seen part of St Peter's Church and the steep roofs of the Mission Hall in Wyld's Lane.

101 *Below left*. The medieval church of St Peter the Great from the south-west, prior to demolition in 1835, painted by H.H. Lines. The church stood at the corner of King Street and St Peter's Street. The church was first mentioned in 969 as dedicated to the saints Perpetua and Felicity.

102 *Below*. The church of St Peter the Great, painted from King Street in 1835 by H.H. Lines prior to demolition. Next to the perpendicular-style tower can be seen the timber-framed wall of the north aisle. Before the 19th century there were substantial amounts of timber-framing in Worcestershire churches. The best local example today is at Besford, near Pershore.

103 A postcard view of the 1890s of St Peter's Street, lined with timber-framed buildings and St Peter's Church in the background. Notice the pinnacles on the tower which were later removed.

104 The rebuilt church of St Peter the Great prior to demolition in 1976. This building of 1836-8 by J. Mills replaced the medieval church, but became structurally unsafe. The parish extended well beyond the city walls and is commemorated in the district of St Peter the Great at the southern end of Bath Road.

105 This early 20th-century picture by A. Troyte-Griffith shows Diglis canal basin, which became the principal wharf area for the city in the early 19th century. The view is dominated by the flour mills, of which only traces now remain after fires and demolitions this century. The canal opened in 1815 and gave access to the river Severn for the Diglis, Sidbury, Blockhouse and Lowesmoor areas.

106 Fort Royal, glimpsed from the grounds of the Commandery in this 19th-century print, marks the steep rise of land to the east of Sidbury. The hill now takes its name from the fortification constructed by the Royalists to defend Worcester from the Parliamentarians during the Civil War. In 1651 this was the scene of the second battle of Worcester. Parts of the earthworks are still in evidence on the hill in Fort Royal Park, which was given to the city in 1913.

The Commandery

107 Sidbury, drawn by H.H. Lines in 1839, showing the three-storey timber-framed house which was demolished to make the drive to the Commandery in 1845. The view shows the canal bridge, and beyond to the left the timber-framed house which stood adjacent to Sidbury Gate, the principal entrance to medieval Worcester from the south. All the buildings on the left-hand side of the street were cleared for road-widening in the 1950s.

108 The Commandery frontage in 1974, before the building was purchased by the City Council. In medieval times it was known as the Hospital of St Wulfstan and its location outside the Sidbury Gate meant that one of its main functions was to provide hospitality for travellers to the city.

109 View from the Commandery canal wing in 1974. Beyond the road is St Peter's Church, which was demolished in 1976. In front of the bridge there is a high wall which screened the Commandery from the canal lock. The wall has been replaced by the present railings and the lock, one of the narrowest in the country, was renovated in 1985. From 1905 to 1973 the Commandery was owned by the Littlebury family, who operated a printing works from the canal wing.

110 This print by F.S. Bayley shows the carriageway which was driven through the medieval Great Hall of the Commandery in 1843. The hall was subsequently restored by the Littleburys in 1954. To the left can be seen the oriel window, kitchen and garden wing. In the foreground are two blind boys; the Commandery was let to the Rev. R.H. Blair, who established a College for the Blind Sons of Gentlemen in 1866, which occupied the premises until 1887.

111 The early 19th-century kitchens of the Commandery were not demolished until the restoration in 1975. This photograph of 1974 shows little change in this part of the building from the previous view. The outline of the kitchen roofs can still be traced on the garden wing.

112 No. 1 Commandery Drive was a separate house created in the 18th century from a wing of the main building. This view, taken in 1976, shows the façade before the restoration during which the 15th-century timber-framing was revealed.

113 No. 1 Commandery Drive from the gardens in 1974. After the Dissolution the Commandery became the country residence of the Wylde family, who were wealthy Worcester clothiers. They extended the building in the late 16th and 17th centuries. The brick-built wing in the centre of the picture encloses earlier timber-framing. Could the upper-floor room have been designed as some kind of gallery?

114 The interior of the garden front attic before restoration in 1974, showing the medieval timbers and curved braces. This part of the hospital building was improved by the Wylde family for more comfortable living in the 17th century, and timbers once visible from the rooms were closed off in the attics.

115 The Commandery from the north west across the canal in 1974 showing the large workshop of Littlebury's printing works. Glass panels in the roof behind remind us that the medieval canal wing was used as industrial premises until the 1970s. This part of the Commandery had been the kitchen and infirmary areas of the hospital, and still contains a room with 15th-century wall-paintings which may have been the infirmary chapel.

116 The workshop area at the Commandery being laid out as a terrace in 1976. Across the canal, the barn and outbuildings are on the line of the city walls. The barn was reconstructed as flats in 1985, and is now known as Amber Wharf.

West of High Street and down to the River Severn

117 Fish Street was bisected by Deansway at the site of the medieval Fishmongers' Hall, which was demolished in 1905. Its large timber-framed gable is the main feature of this view by E.A. Phipson, dated 1902. Fish Street was known as Corviser Street in the medieval period and was the area occupied by cordwainers or leather-workers. The buildings in view further east along the street still survive today.

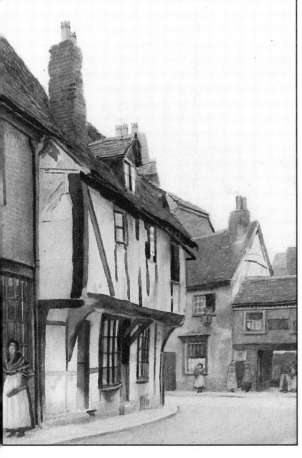

118 Birdport was painted in 1904 by E.A. Phipson. It ran to the north from Copenhagen Street, along what is now Deansway by the police station. Most of the timber-framed and brick houses were demolished in the 1930s.

119 At the north end of Birdport, formerly Britport, was the junction with Grope Lane, painted by E.A. Phipson in 1898. It has been suggested that the name Birdport means the street going towards the British (or towards Wales) from the Saxon town.

120 An unusual view of the north side of Copenhagen Street, painted by E.A. Phipson in 1904. Copenhagen Street was renamed after the Battle of Copenhagen in 1801, but was formerly known as Cooken Street, a name which appears to have connections with the ducking stool. The low wall and trees mark the entrance to St Andrew's churchyard, and in the background, the junction with Birdport is just visible.

121 St Andrew's Church and Copenhagen Street from the river Severn in 1912, by K.J. Minchin. The spire of St Andrew's Church still survives and is known as the Glover's Needle, as this area was largely occupied by people engaged in gloving from the 17th to 20th centuries. However, the streets have been cleared since the 1920s and the buildings seen here have been largely demolished.

122 The rear of Copenhagen Street from St Andrew's churchyard in the 1930s prior to clearance.

123 This fine 18th-century view of All Hallows shows All Saints' Church behind a row of houses. In the foreground is a conduit. All Hallows was the first open market place to be reached across the medieval bridge and had its origins as a cattle market serving the west of the county.

124 A house in All Saints' Passage beside the church is shown in this view by E.A. Phipson, dated 1892. The right-hand support for the timber-framed porch has been replaced by a twisted trunk—notice the mortice hole for the original timber.

125 Cottages behind All Saints' Church, painted in 1904 by E.A. Phipson. The area between the church and the river was a network of courts and alley-ways, cleared during the middle part of this century.

126 & 127 *Left*. All Saints' Church was rebuilt in 1739-42, incorporating the medieval tower base. In the 19th century, it was decided to clear the surrounding houses in All Hallows to open up a view of the north side. The house at the west end of the terrace is shown with a Flemish-style gable of the 17th century.

128 *Right*. This photograph shows the interior of All Saints' Church in September 1904. Next to the woman, a Miss Agape Parker, is the chained bible and 18th-century wrought-iron sword rest. The sword rest would have once been located in the mayor's pews, and the ceremonial sword placed there, when the mayor attended the church. The sword rest has been resited at the east end of the nave.

129 *Below*. Newport Street led from the medieval bridge to All Hallows. Although it was bypassed by Bridge Street and the new bridge in 1781, but many of these medieval buildings survived into this century. This view by E.A. Phipson was painted in 1905.

130 Dolday was the most north-western street of medieval Worcester. It was largely occupied by people associated with the cloth industry. The street fell into decline from the 18th century, and this view of 1902 by E.A. Phipson shows it prior to clearance. Today only the lower part of the street still exists as a busy traffic route.

131 Dolday in 1931 looking towards Broad Street.

The Cross, Foregate Street and into the north

132 The Cross. To the north of the High Street is The Cross. This street was dominated by a cross in medieval times and was the traditional commercial centre for the city. This view, painted by H. Romer in June 1934, shows the 18th- and 19th-century buildings around St Nicholas' Church, which was rebuilt with its fine tower in the 1730s. The scene is little changed today apart from the traffic.

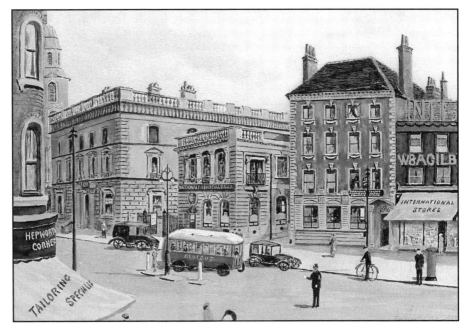

133 A busy postcard view of The Cross in the early 1900s, looking towards the railway bridge in Foregate Street.

134 To the north of The Cross, the site of the Foregate marked the northern boundary of the medieval city. The large gate spanned the street at this point and a suburb extended beyond along the present Foregate Street. This photograph shows the group of fine 18th- and 19th-century buildings at the south end of Foregate Street as they were in 1975. Notice that the traffic was still able to travel south.

135 An early 19th-century print of Foregate Street looking south towards St Nicholas' Church. In 1556 Leland described the street as 'a long fayre surburbe by Northe without the Fore-Gate', but after serious damage during the Civil War the area fell into decline to be rebuilt as the fine Georgian street seen here.

136 A bazaar held at the Shire Hall to raise funds for a new natural history museum is recorded in this print of *c.*1845. The first natural history museum was founded in 1833 in Angel Street by Sir Charles Hastings, but moved to larger premises in Foregate Street in 1836, before it became part of the City Museum in the Victoria Institute in 1896.

137 The public library and Hastings Museum occupied this building on the site of the present Odeon Cinema from 1836 until the Victoria Institute opened in 1896. By the 1880s it was clear that Worcester needed a large, more up-to-date museum and in 1884 a campaign was started to combine a museum, library and school of art and science in one building.

138, 139 & 140 The site of the Victoria Institute, Foregate Street, was occupied by these Georgian houses, including Acacia House, until the 1890s. The turning visible beside Acacia House in 140 (*below*) is Taylors lane. The rendered building in 139 (*below left*) still exists on the forecourt of the Shire Hall.

Elevation · to · Foregate · Street ·

141 The Foregate Street elevation of the Victoria Institute, designed by J.W. Simpson and Milner Allen in 1896. The museum and art gallery are on the first floor, and the library occupies the ground floor. The first city library was founded in Angel Place in 1790, before moving to Pierpoint Street in 1831, to Foregate Street in 1881, from where it was moved to expanded accommodation at the Victoria Institute.

142 *Above*. The art gallery in the Victoria Institute hung with oil paintings in the early part of the 20th century. These are not part of the present collection and appear to be a temporary exhibition reflecting the municipal taste of the period.

143 *Above right*. Part of the porcelain collection of the City Museum on display in the early 20th century.

144 *Right*. This 19th-century print shows the Shire Hall beyond iron railings and before the erection of the statue of Queen Victoria in 1887. The Shire Hall was built in 1834-5 to a Grecian design by Charles Day and Henry Rowe. A major refurbishment was completed in 1995.

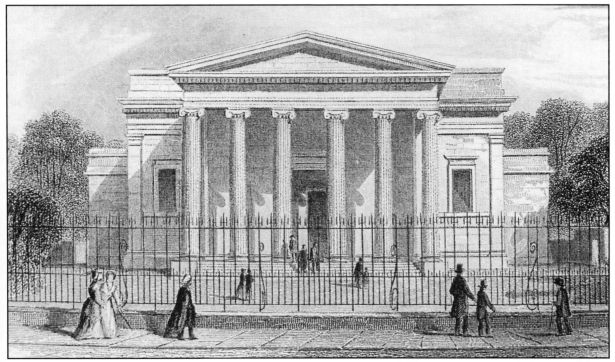

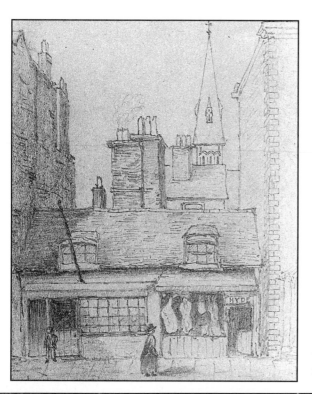

145 The continuation northwards of this suburb is known as The Tything. Once part of the parish of Claines, it was lined with small cottages which were replaced by larger houses in the 18th century. These cottages stood on the site of No. 59 until the late 19th century. By the time of their demolition, they were dwarfed by surrounding buildings. In the background of this 1892 drawing is the spire of the Presbyterian church in Castle Street, built in 1865 and demolished in 1965.

146 77 The Tything in 1908, then the shop of S.G. Gregory. During the late 19th century, as the residential areas expanded further away from the city centre, The Tything took on a more commercial rôle.

147 The *Saracen's Head* in The Tything had a large bowling green behind during the 19th century, but this has since been built over. Sansome Walk, which runs parallel to The Tything and Foregate Street, was established in the 18th century as a promenade for this elegant suburb. The obelisk from the north end can still be found in the grounds of St Oswald's Hospital.

148 Britannia Square was developed between 1818 and the 1830s on open fields, with a terrace as well as detached and semi-detached houses. The centre plot was filled with a large house called Springfield, seen here as painted by H. Romer in 1937. During excavations for the cellars in 1829, masonry and about fifty Roman coins were discovered. Debate continues on the purpose of the site in Roman times, but both a fortification and a temple have been suggested.

149 & 150 Little London runs south-east from Upper Tything around the grounds of the Royal Grammar School and the site of the nunnery of Whistones. The name was generally given to a group of buildings in a rural area and may be associated with the late medieval tiling industry here. In 1903, when E.A. Phipson painted the street, it had groups of attractive cottages. These were later demolished, as shown in the undated snapshot below.

Outer Worcester

151 On the west side of the river Severn the suburb of St John's was linked to the medieval bridge by Tybridge Street. Few pre-20th-century buildings remain in Tybridge Street or Hylton Road which runs alongside the river. This photograph, taken *c*.1930, shows the *Bear Inn* on the junction of the two roads.

152 St John's remained outside the city boundary until 1837. In medieval times it was a busy road junction with timber-framed houses clustering around the church. By the 19th century it had expanded considerably with large houses in spacious grounds, especially along Henwick Road, and many streets and lanes of small cottages. These Victorian cottages in Grosvenor Walk are shown prior to renovation in 1979.

153 Church Walk takes its name from St Clement's Church. The medieval church of St Clement stood at the west end of Dolday, by the river, but the parish lay on the west bank around Henwick. After centuries of flooding, a new church was built in Henwick Road in 1822. It is an extraordinary building in a neo-Norman style and can be seen across the site of the cottages at the west end of Tybridge Street. This photograph was taken in 1977, before flats and houses were built on the site.

154 The former St Clement's School is overshadowed by the Tybridge Street flats in this 1977 photograph.

155 The St John's end of Bransford Road is sometimes still referred to as The Green. Each year in the middle ages a fair was held here on the Friday before Palm Sunday, a custom which was revived in 1770. There were several timber-framed cottages along the road, some of which feature in this painting by E.A. Phipson of 1910. Little now remains.

156 The manor house of Hardwick in St John's, known as the Great House. This painting was presented to Worcester City Museum in 1903, some two years before the demolition of this house which stood on Malvern Road, St John's. The site is commemorated by the name Great House Road.

157 St George's Lane in Barbourne contained several pre-Victorian houses and cottages. These have now all but disappeared, but this view painted by E.A. Phipson in 1905 shows some which survived until this century. Barbourne is a residential suburb to the north of the city, formerly in the parish of Claines. St George's Church was built in 1893-5 to designs by Sir Aston Webb.

158 Pitchcroft Lane runs from the north end of Pitchcroft. This view of 1892 by E.A. Phipson shows a timber-framed house standing next to the 19th-century terraces. Horse-racing has taken place on Pitchcroft since the early 18th century—it is first mentioned in 1718.

159 The Shrubbery was home to the Smith Hanson family, Worcester textile merchants, in the late 19th century. The house was demolished and replaced by Shrubbery Avenue in the first years of the 20th century.

160 *Left*. The riverside by Pitchcroft in the early 20th century, with passengers alighting from the Dog and Duck Ferry. The trees to the left flank the racecourse.

161 *Right*. This painting, possibly by H. Holland, shows the former tower of the waterworks in Barbourne. The works were built in 1770, and water was taken from the river Severn to be pumped from this tower into wooden pipes to supply the city. It became redundant when the new waterworks were built in 1856, and was finally demolished in the 1960s.

162 *Below*. Gheluvelt Park, Barbourne, in the early 1920s. The Worcestershire Regiment's heroism at the Battle of Gheluvelt in Belgium in 1914 is commemorated in this park.

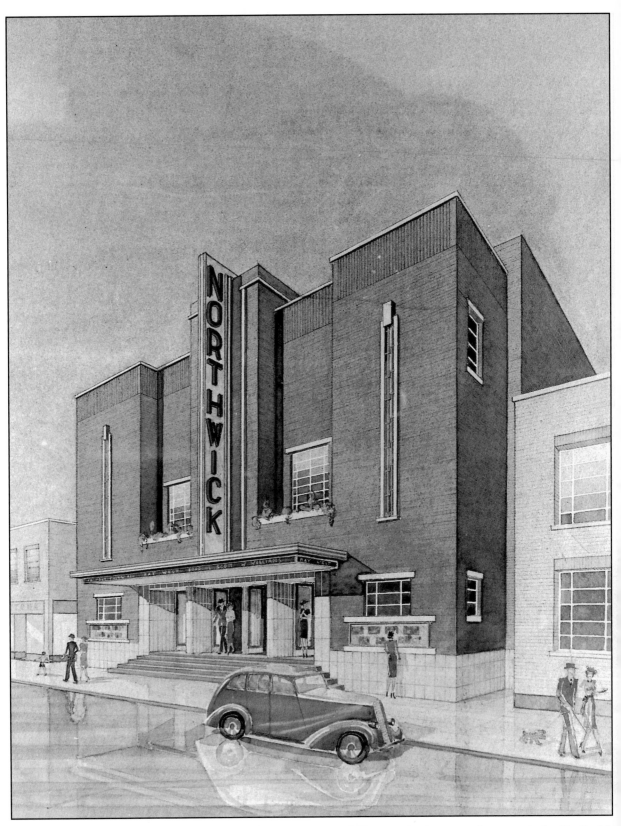

163 An artist's impression of the Northwick Cinema. The last of Worcester's cinemas to be opened, the Northwick was built in 1938 with interior designs by John Alexander. Behind this plain façade is an extraordinary art-deco interior which has recently been restored.

164 Perdiswell Hall was built for the Wakeman family in 1788 by George Byfield. Thomas Wakeman was mayor of Worcester in 1761 and owned much land in Claines. The Hall was sold in about 1860, and was eventually burnt down and demolished in 1956.

165 The Old Turnpike near the Battenhall Road junction of London Road, was the start of the main overland route from Worcester to London. Weekly mail coaches ran from the city to the capital in the 18th century. Extensive suburbs developed in this area on Green Hill and Red Hill in the 18th and 19th centuries.

166 The show of the Royal Agricultural Society at Worcester took place at Battenhall in 1863. Medieval Battenhall was a deer park for the priory of Worcester, and passed through a succession of families after the Dissolution. Queen Elizabeth I hunted here during her visit in 1575. Battenhall Road was created as an entrance to the show and developed as a residential suburb in the late 19th century.

Bibliography and References

Allely, L., and Phillips, C., *St Clement's* (1969)

Allies, J., *Antiquities of Worcestershire*, 2nd edn. (1856)

Atkin, M., *The Civil War in Worcestershire* (1995)

Baker, N.J., 'The urban churches of Worcester', *Transactions of the Worcestershire Archaeological Society*, 3rd series, vol. 7 (1980)

Baker, N.J., Dalwood, C.H., Holt, R., Mundy, C.F., and Taylor, G., 'From Roman to medieval Worcester: development and planning in the Anglo-Saxon city', *Antiquity*, vol. 66 (1992)

Barker, P.A. (ed.), 'The origins of Worcester', *Transactions of the Worcestershire Archaeological Society*, 3rd series, vol. 2 (1970)

Barker, P.A., *A short architectural history of Worcester Cathedral*, Worcester Cathedral Publications, No. 2 (1994)

Barker, P.A., Cubberley, A.L., Crowfoot, E., and Radford, C.A.R., 'Two burials under the refectory at Worcester Cathedral', *Medieval Archaeology*, vol. 18 (1974)

Bassett, S., 'Churches in Worcester before and after the conversion of the Anglo-Saxons', *Antiquaries Journal*, vol. 69, part 2 (1989)

Beardsmore, C., 'Documentary evidence for the history of Worcester City defences', *Transactions of the Worcestershire Archaeological Society*, 3rd series, vol. 7 (1980)

Burnham, B.C., and Wacher, J., *The small towns of Roman Britain* (1990)

Carver, M.O.H., 'The site and settlements at Worcester', *Transactions of the Worcestershire Archaeological Society*, 3rd series, vol. 7 (1980)

Carver, M.O.H., 'The excavation of three medieval craftsmen's tenements in Sidbury Worcester, 1976', *Transactions of the Worcestershire Archaeological Society*, 3rd series, vol. 7 (1980)

Cobb, G., *English Cathedrals: The Forgotten Centuries* (1980)

Dalwood, C.H., 'Salvage recording of a medieval stone undercroft and cellars at 84-85 High Street, Worcester', *Transactions of the Worcestershire Archaeological Society*, 3rd series, vol. 13 (1992)

Dalwood, C.H., Buteux, V.A., and Jackson, R.A., 'Interim report on excavations at Deansway, Worcester 1988-89', *Transactions of the Worcestershire Archaeological Society*, 3rd series, vol. 13 (1992)

Dalwood, C.H., Buteux, V.A., and Darlington, J., 'Excavations at Farrier Street and other sites in the Foregate suburb, Worcester, 1989-90', *Transactions of the Worcestershire Archaeological Society*, 3rd series, vol. 14 (1994)

Darlington, J., and Evans, J., 'Roman Sidbury, Worcester: Excavations 1959-1989', *Transactions of the Worcestershire Archaeological Society*, 3rd series, vol. 13 (1992)

Dowty, M., *Worcester, wish you were still here* (1993)

Dowty, W., and Dowty, M., *Worcester in old photographs* (1986)

Frost, H., and Cook, W., *Royal Worcester Porcelain and the Dyson Perrins Collection* (1993)

Green, V., *The history and antiquities of the City and suburbs of Worcester* (1796)

Guy, C., 'Excavations at Worcester Cathedral 1981-1991', *Transactions of the Worcestershire Archaeological Society*, 3rd series, vol. 14 (1994)

Gwilliam, H.W., *Old Worcester: People and Places* (1993)

Hallett, M., *Worcester Cathedral: A Grand View* (1987)

Haynes, C., and Haynes, M., *Old Worcester as seen through the Camera* (1986)

Haynes, C., Haynes, M., and Adlam, B., *Yesterday's Town; the changing face of Worcester* (1978)

Hillaby, J., 'The Worcester jewry 1158-1290: portrait of a lost community', *Transactions of the Worcestershire Archaeological Society*, 3rd series, vol. 12 (1990)

Hughes, P., 'Houses and Property in Post-Reformation Worcester', *Transactions of the Worcestershire Archaeological Society*, 3rd series, vol. 7 (1980)

Hughes, P., and Molyneux, N., *Friar Street* (1984)

Jones, R., *Porcelain in Worcester 1751-1951, an Illustrated Social History* (1993)

Knowles, J.M., 'College Green in the 19th century', in Barker, P., and Guy, C. (eds.), *Worcester Cathedral: Report of the Second Annual Symposium on the Precinct* (1992)

Latta, C. (*et al.*), *The Commandery* (1981)

Lubin, H., *The Worcester Pilgrim*, Worcester Cathedral Publications, No. 1 (1990)

Molyneux, N., 'A late medieval stone building in Angel Street', *Transactions of the Worcestershire Archaeological Society*, 3rd series, vol. 7 (1980)

Molyneux, N., 'The Edgar Tower, Worcester', in Barker, P., and Guy, C. (eds.), *Worcester Cathedral: Report of the Second Annual Symposium on the Precinct* (1992)

Mundy, C.F., 'Excavations at Blackfriars, Worcester', *West Midlands Archaeology*, vol. 29 (1986)

Noake, J., *The Monastery and Cathedral of Worcester* (1886)

Owen, B.R., *Worcester in old postcards* (1992)

Pevsner, N., *The Buildings of England: Worcestershire* (1968)

Roslington, C. (ed.), *The King's School, Worcester and a history of the site* (1994)

Stafford, T., *Worcester as it was* (1977)

Whitehead, D., 'John Gwynn R.A. and the Building of Worcester Bridge 1769-86', *Transactions of the Worcestershire Archaeological Society*, 3rd series, vol. 8 (1972)

Whitehead, D., *The Book of Worcester* (1976)

Whitehead, D., *Urban Renewal and Suburban Growth: The Shaping of Georgian Worcester* (1989)

Whitehead, D., 'The Georgian churches of Worcester', *Transactions of the Worcestershire Archaeological Society*, 3rd series, vol. 13 (1992)

Willis-Bund, J.W. (ed.), *History of the County of Worcestershire II*, Victory County History (1906)

Worcester City Council, *Worcester 800, a celebration* (1989)

Index

Roman numbers refer to pages in the introduction, and arabic numerals to individual illustrations.

d'Abitot, Urse, xx, 5
Acacia House, 138-40
Aethelbald, King, xvii
Aethelflaed, xvii, xviii
Aethelred, xviii
Albion Mills, xxx
All Hallows, xix, 123, 126-7, 129
All Saints' Church, xviii, xix, 6, 123, 125-8
All Saints' Passage, 124
almshouses, xxiv, xxix, 68, 73, 91
Angel Court, 96
Angel Place, xix
Arboretum, xxix

Barr, Flight & Barr, xxviii, 27
Battenhall, xix, 166
Bear Inn, 151
Beauchamp family, xix, xxiv
Beauchamp, William, xxii
Benedictines, xix
Berhtwulf, King, xvii
Berrows Journal, xxvii
Birdport, 118, 119
Birmingham and Worcester Canal, xi, xxix, xxx
Bishop's Palace, xxi
Blackfriars, xv, xxiv
Blair, Rev. R.H., 110
Blockhouse, 13, 80, 82, 90
Blue Coat School, xxvii
Bosel, Bishop, xvi
breweries, xxx
bridge, medieval, 20, 129
Britannia Square, xv, 2, 148
Butts, The, xxix

castle, xx, xxii, 5
cathedral, xix, xxi, xxii, xxiii, xxviii, 7, 12, 27, 31, 32, 35
Cathedral Close, xii, xiii, xiv, xvi
Cathedral Precincts, 34
Chamberlain, Robert, xxviii
Chamberlain's factory, 99
chapter house, 38, 40, 46
Chapter Meadows, 31
church, floating, 25
Cinderella Shoes, xxx, 91
City Arcade, 62
City Gaol, xxix, 68
city gates, xxiii, 107

city wall, xviii, xxi, xxii, xxvi, 87-94
City Walls Road, 89, 90
Civil War, xxvi, xxvii, 106
cloth manufacture, xxv
clothing manufacture, xxvii
College for the Blind Sons of Gentlemen, 110
College Grates, 59
College Green, 49, 50
College Hall, 47, 48
College Precincts, 51
College Street, 52
College Yard, 34
Commandery, the, xxiv, xxvi, 92, 93, 107-116
Commandery Drive, 112, 113
Congregational School, xxviii
Copenhagen Street, 120, 121, 122
Cornmarket, xii, 78, 90
County Cricket Club, 31
County Cricket Ground, xxxi
County Prison, xxix
County Record Office, 60
Cripplegate House, 8
Cripplegate Park, xxxi
Cross, The, 132, 133
Crown Hotel, xxix
crypt, 37

Danes, xx
Davies, John, Rector of St Clement's, 25
Deanery, 44, 45, 118
Deansway, xv, xix, xxv
Derby, Earl of, xxii
Diglis, xi, xii, xv, xvii, xxix, 10, 11, 28, 29
Diglis canal basin, 105
Diglis Hotel, 88
Dissolution, xxiv
Dog and Duck Ferry, 160
Dolday, 130, 131
Domesday Book, xxi

Edgar Street, 50, 95
Edgar Tower, xii, 50
education, xxx, 83
Elgar, Sir Edward, 59, 79
Elizabeth I, xxv, 73, 166

Farrier Street, xv

Fishmongers' Hall, 117
Fish Street, 117
floods, 16, 17
Florence, of Worcester, xx
Foregate, 134
Foregate Street, 134, 138-41
Fort Royal Hill, xxvi, xxvii, 106
Fort Royal Park, xxxi
Fountain Inn, 98
Fownes factory, xxvii, 81, 92
Friar Street, xii, 58, 66, 68, 69
Friary Mall, xiv
Frog Brook, xi, xiv, xxiii

Gheluvelt Park, xxxi, 162
glove-making, xxvii, xxviii, xxx, 81, 92, 130
Golden Lion, The, xxv
Grainger's, xxviii
Great House, 156
Green, the, Bransford Road, 155
Gregory, S.H., shop, 146
Greyfriars, xxiii, xxiv
Greyfriars, house, 67
Grosvenor Walk, 152
Guesten Hall, 42, 43
Guild of the Holy Trinity, xxiv
Guildhall, xxiv, xxix, 62, 64, 65
Gwynne, John, xxix, 23
Gwynne's bridge, 21, 22

Hadley, James, factory, xxviii
Hardy and Padmore, xxx
Harthacnut, King, xx
Hastings, salt trow, 16
Hastings, Sir Charles, xxviii, xxx
Hastings, Museum, 137
Heaberht, xvii
health, xxxi
Heenan and Froude, xxx
Henry II, xxii
Henry III, xxii, xxiv
High Street, xxi, 59, 60
Hill Evans Vinegar Works, xxx
hopmarket, xxix, 75
Hwicce, xvi

industry, xxiv, xxv, xxx
infirmary, xxviii, 3,
infirmary, monastic, 32, 33
iron industry, xiv, xv

James I, xxvi
James's fish shop, 72
Jewish quarter, xxiv
John, King, xxii

King Street, 99, 100-102
King's School, xxii, 31, 47, 49

Larkworthy & Co., J.L., xxx
Laslett, William, xxix
Laslett's Almshouses, 68
Lea and Perrins, xxx
library, xxx, 137, 141
Lich Gate, 53, 54, 58
Lich Street, 56, 57, 58
Little London, 149-50
Little Park Street, 84
Littlebury family, 109
Littlebury's printing works, 115
Lock Street, 83
Locke works, xxviii
Lowesmoor, 13, 76, 85
Lychgate centre, xiii, xxi
Lyppard, xix

Mackenzie and Holland, xxx
Maddox, Bishop Isaac, xxviii
Manor Farm, xix
market, xviii, xix, 63
Market Hall, 62, 63
medieval town, xviii, 1
Metal Castings, xxx
Mildred, Bishop, xvii
Mining Engineering Co., The, xxx
Mission Hall, 100
Mortimer, Hugh, xxii
Mucklow, William, xxv
museum, 94, 136, 141

Nash House, 70
Nash, John, Mayor, 70
New Road, 17
New Street, xii, 70, 90
Newport Street, 129
Nicholson, organ, 79
Norman Conquest, xix
Normans, xx
Northwick, xix
Northwick Cinema, 163

Odeon Cinema, xxxi, 137
Old Palace, 27
Oswald, Bishop, xix

Padmore, Richard, 62
Parker, Miss Agape, 128
Perdiswell golf-course, xiii
Perdiswell Hall, 164
Pitchcroft, xi, xxix, xxxi, 9, 158, 160
plague, xxvi
Portabello Tea Gardens, 9
Powick, xxvii
Powick Church, 30

Powick Mills, xxxi
prehistoric settlement, xii, xiii
prison, xxii, xxix
Public Hall, The, 79
Punch Bowl Inn, 53

Queen Elizabeth House, xxv, 73, 74

racecourse, xxix
railway, xxx
rebellion, xx
Richard I, xxiv
Romans, xiii, xiv, xv, 148
Royal Agricultural Society show, 166
Royal Grammar School, xxiv
Royal Worcester Porcelain Works, xix, xxviii, 11, 27, 98, 99

St Alban's Church, xvi, xvii, xix, xxviii
St Andrew's Church, xix, xxviii, 8, 120, 121
St Clement, church of, xxi, 153
St Clement's School, 154
St Cuthbert's Church, xix
St George's Lane, 157
St George's Roman Catholic Church, 75
St Godwald (St Gudwal), xix
St Helen's Church, xv, xvi, xix, 60, 61
St John's Church, xxiv
St John's, suburb, xi, xix, xxiv, xxvii, xxix, 151-2
St Margaret's Church, xvii, xix
St Martin's Church, xix, xxi, 89
St Mary's Church, xix
St Michael, Church of, xxi, 51, 53, 55
St Nicholas, Church of, xix, xxi, 6, 132, 135
St Paul's Church, 82
St Peter's Church, xv, xix, 100-103, 109
St Peter the Great, xix, 104
St Peter's Junior School, 94
St Peter's Sunday School, 83
St Swithun's Church, xix
St Wulfstan's Hospital, xix, xxiv, 108, *see also* Commandery, the
salmon fishing, 18
Sansome Fields, xxix, xxxi
Sansome Street, 75, 76
Saracen's Head, 147
Saxons, xix
Severn, river, xi, xii, xxv, xxix, 12, 16, 19, 26, 29, 88, 121
Severn Street, 97, 98
Shambles, The, 71, 72
Shire Hall, 136, 144
shoe-making, xxx
Shrub Hill Road, 86

Shrubbery, The, 159
Sidbury, xv, 95-107
Sigley's China, 63
Sigley's sweet factory, 80
Silver Street, 76
slum clearance, xxxi, 69
Smith-Carrington, Mayor, 74
Smith Hanson, 159
South Quay, 15, 19
spa, xxvii
Springfield, 148
Star Hotel, xxix
Stephen, King, xxii
Studdert-Kennedy, Rev. G.A. ('Woodbine Willie'), 82

Tallow Hill, xxviii, xxix
Teme, river, 29
Theodore, Archbishop, xvi
Three Choirs Festival, 79
tollhouses, 23
tolls, table of, 24
Tower Manufacturing Co., xxx
Town Ditch, 76
Townsend's flour mill, 91
Trinity, the, xii, 77
Trinity Hospital, 73, 77
Turnpike, Old, 165
Tybridge Street flats, 154
Tything, The, 145-7

Unicorn Hotel, xxix

Victoria Institute, 138-142
Vulcan Iron Works, xxx

Waerfirth, Bishop, xvii, xviii
Wakeman, Thomas, 164
Wall, Dr., xxviii, 5, 27
Warmstry House, 27
Warndon Court Farm, xix
Water Gate, 36
waterworks, Barbourne, 161
Whiteladies, xxiv
Wick, xix
William, of Blois, Bishop, xxiii
Worcester City Museum, 73, 74, 136, 143
Worcester Exhibition, 86
Worcester General Infirmary, xxviii
Worcester Porcelain Works, xxviii, xxx
Worcester Power Station, xxxi
Worcester, S.S., 15
workhouse, xxviii
Wulfstan, Bishop, xx, xxi, xxiii
Wyatt's Almshouses, 91
Wylde, Thomas, xxvi
Wylde family, 113

Yarranton, Andrew, xiv